HUMAN RESOURCES MANAGEMENT

Pratibha Tripathi

Qurate
quratebooks.com

HUMAN RESOURCES MANAGEMENT
Pratibha Tripathi

Published in 2024

© Published by

Qurate
qaratebooks.com

Qurate Books Pvt. Ltd.
Goa 403523, India
www.quratebooks.com
Tel: 1800-210-6527, Email: info@quratebooks.com

ISBN: 978-93-58988-93-2

Unit 1-

Introduction to HRM and HRD, Concept of HRM, Objectives, Process, HRM Versus Personnel Management, HRM versus HRD, Objective of HRD, Focus of HRD System, Structure of HRD System, Role of HRD, Manpower.

Unit 2-

Human Resource Policies and Strategies - Introduction, Role of HR in Strategic Management, HR Policies and Procedure, HR Program, Developing HR Policies and Strategies, Strategic Control, Types of Strategic Control, Operational Control System, Functional and Grand Strategies, Strategy Factors.

Unit 3-

Human Resource Procurement and Mobility, Productivity and Improvement, Job Analysis and Job Design, Work Measurement, Ergonomics. Human Resource Planning- Objectives, Activities, Manpower Requirement Process, Recruitment and Selection, Career Planning and Development, Training Methods, Basic Concept of Performance Appraisal, Promotion and Transfer.

Unit 4-

Employee Compensation, Wage Policy, Wage Determination, Wage Boar, Factors Affecting Wages and Salary, Systems of Payments, Job Evaluation, Components of Wages/salary - DA, Incentives, Bonus, Fringe Benefits, etc., Minimum Wages Act 1948, Workmen Compensation Act 1923, Payment of Bonus Act 1965.

Unit 5-

Employee Relations, Discipline and Grievance Handling, Types of Trade Unions, Problems of Trade Unions.

Unit -I

HUMAN RESOURCE MANAGEMENT

Human resource management is the strategic approach to nurturing and supporting employees and ensuring a positive workplace environment. Its functions vary across different businesses and industries, but typically include recruitment, compensation and benefits, training and development, and employee relations.

The job of an HR manager can be broken out into three major roles:

1. **Administrator**

   Running payroll, writing job descriptions, creating workplace policies and procuring benefits packages are typical of HR administration.

2. **Change manager**

   HR professionals must monitor regulations and communicate policy or procedural changes with employees to help support compliance.

3. **Personnel manager**

   Managing people entails resolving conflicts, overseeing training and development, and fostering employee engagement.

The five main areas of HR?

HR professionals perform many activities in the pursuit of employee well-being and organizational stability, but their responsibilities generally lie within five main areas:

1. **Recruitment and staffing** - identifying talent gaps, acquiring applicants, arbitrating contracts, maintaining ethical hiring practices
2. **Compensation and benefits** - determining pay scales, approving raises, negotiating benefits packages
3. **Training and development** - onboarding new hires, making educational opportunities available
4. **Compliance and safety** - monitoring legislative changes, implementing safety measures, processing workers' compensation claims
5. **Employee relations** - resolving employee conflicts, addressing harassment or abuse allegations, working with union leaders

Seven functions of HR?

Over the years, HR has evolved from a personnel department engaged largely in administration to a strategic partner that works closely with management teams on organizational development. It's seven key functions today include:

1. Strategic planning
2. Recruitment
3. Training and development
4. Compensation and benefits
5. Policy creation
6. Employee and labor relations
7. Risk management

HR compliance?

HR compliance means keeping an organization from violating the growing number of employment laws enacted by federal, state and local governments. This responsibility requires HR professionals to monitor and understand regulatory requirements, enforce policies, **classify workers** correctly, practice fair hiring practices and provide a safe work environment, among other tasks.

This guide is intended to be used as a starting point in analyzing an employer's HR obligations and is not a comprehensive resource of requirements. It offers practical information concerning the subject matter and is provided with the understanding that ADP is not rendering legal or tax advice or other professional services.

Examples of human resource management objectives

Here are some examples of other objectives that HR managers may make:

1. To develop a safe and positive work culture
2. To provide incentives to retain key talent and maintain a stable work environment
3. To develop efficient communication methods between departments to ensure effective collaboration
4. To provide high-quality and consistent training opportunities for new team members
5. To manage payroll efficiently and minimize any challenges with the software
6. To increase recruitment fairs at nearby colleges and universities
7. To maintain employee morale by maintaining clean and attractive work facilities
8. To create resources and tools that enable workforce empowerment

9. To ensure that all company HR policies meet compliance with local rules and regulations
10. To integrate a person's individual goals with the goals of the department and organization
11. To improve performance tracking to ensure high output from everyone in the company
12. To create engaging events to increase company morale and facilitate communication between departments
13. To develop communication methods where people can provide honest feedback about the organization
14. To consistently assess training standards and analyze the effectiveness of current training and development programs
15. To hire qualified individuals in leadership positions to ensure fair and effective leadership throughout all company departments

Everything you need to know about the various definitions of human resource management. Human resource management is a systematic process of managing people working in the organization.

Human resource management is a managerial process of acquiring and engaging the required workforce, appropriate for the job and concerned with developing, maintenance and utilization of work force.

According to Decenzo and Robbins, "HRM is concerned with the people dimension" in management.

Since every organization is made up of people, acquiring their services, developing their skills, motivating them to higher levels of performance and ensuring that they continue to maintain their commitment to the organization is essential to achieve organisational objectives. This is true, regardless of the type of organization - government, business, education, health or social action.

Human Resource Management (HRM) is that part of management process which develops and manages the human element of the enterprise considering their resourcefulness in terms of total knowledge, skills, creative abilities, talents, aptitudes and potentialities for effectively contributing to the organisational objectives.

The most important asset of the organization is its employees, so the prime responsibility of management is to manage human resource in effective manner.

The basic function of management is to bring employees and organization on the same platform in order to meet the individual goals as well as organizational goals at the same time.

The management of human resources is an art because the sequences of growth and changes that occurs in life.:

Learn about the definitions of human resource management propounded by various authors, management thinkers and institutions.

Human Resource Management Definitions by Different Authors, Management Thinkers and Various Institutions

Human Resource Management Definitions – Given by Eminent Authors Like: Pigors and Myers, Byars and Rue, Ivancevich and Glueck

People at work at different levels and departments of the organisation plus their inherent abilities, acquired knowledge and skills as exemplified in their talents and aptitudes.

Human resources are also identified by other terms like 'personnel', 'people at work' 'human assets' and 'human capital'. Human assets are intangible as they exist within the human resources. Sumantra Ghoshal has used the term 'human capital' to represent human resources. Human capital consists of intellectual capital, social capital and emotional capital.

Managing people at work in various settings. In general, human resource means people. Human Resource Management refers to, Michael J. Jucius has defined human resources as "a whole consisting of inter-related, inter¬dependent and interacting physiological, psychological, sociological and ethical components".

Definitions:

Pigors and Myers – "It is basically a method of developing potentialities of employees so that they feel maximum satisfaction of their work and give their best efforts to the organization".

Byars and Rue – "Human resource management encompasses those activities designed to provide for and coordinate the human resources of an organization Human resource functions refer to those tasks and duties performed in organizations to provide for and coordinate human resources".

Ivancevich and Glueck – "Human resource management is the function performed in organizations' that facilitate the most effective use of people Objectives & Nature of Human Resource Management

Human capital is a critical aspect of modern business. These two words describe employees as a resource or asset beneficial to the company. However, people usually aren't as simple and come with a bunch of individual and group requirements. This is where human resource management or HRM comes in. HRM is a practice that involves recruiting, hiring, training, and managing an organisation's employees. Over the years, the nature of human resource management has evolved from being a function under other areas of management to holding its position as a key pillar in the overall business strategy.

Human resource management is all about having the right people, with the right capabilities, in the right place, at the right time!

Human resource management can be your ideal job if you like to approach and encourage people. The tasks of an HR manager do not include only hiring and firing. It also involves activities such as job design, employee relations, overseeing payroll, and managing staff benefits. To successfully carry out your duties, you must know the nature of human resource management and its objectives. However, first, let's understand what human resource management is.

Understanding Human Resource Management

In today's competitive business world, no organisation can imagine surviving without a team of efficient employees or human resources. To retain this efficient pool of employees, it is important to manage human resources effectively. Human resource management is defined as the process of acquiring, recruiting, and retaining employees in an organisation.

HRM serves multiple essential purposes in an organisation for the growth of employees and the company. It is essential for both an organisation and its employees. For an organisation, HRM aims to maintain a positive work culture and fulfil the organisational goals. For employees, HRM provides them with a direction to achieve organisational goals, motivating them to perform more efficiently in the future.

Nature of Human Resource Management

Human resource management brings people together in an organisation. Why? To make sure both individual and organisation goals are fulfilled! The following features characterise the nature of human resource management:-

- **Managerial Proces**

  Human resource management is a vital part of management that includes planning, organising, staffing, directing, and controlling human resources to achieve organisational success. It is a managerial process that effectively utilises human resources to attain organisational goals and objectives.

- **Both Art and Science**

  Human resource management is a mixture of both art and science. It is an art as it deals with qualitative attributes like creativity, knowledge, skills, and talent of the personnel. In simple words, HRM is the art of getting things done by others effectively. HRM is a science as it requires different scientific techniques for activities like recruitment, selection, training, and appraisal of employees.

- **Pervasive Force**

  Human resource management, being an inherent part of an organisation, is pervasive in nature. It means that HRM is present in different functional areas of management, like finance, marketing, and production, in all commercial and non-commercial enterprises. Everyone in the organisation, from the top to the lowest level, must perform HRM functions regularly.

- **Improve Employee Relations**

  "In order to build a rewarding employee experience, you need to understand what matters most to your people." – Julie Bevacqua.

Human resource management is concerned with building healthy relationships between employees at various organisational levels. Every individual has different needs, goals, and expectations. HRM deals with these individual factors and motivates employees to reach their maximum potential. Moreover, it creates an organisational culture that fosters learning and growth.

- **People-Centred**

  The nature of human resource management is people-centred and relevant in all types of organisations. It is concerned with every employee from the top to the bottom level. HRM value people both as individuals and as a group. Furthermore, it encourages people to develop their full potential and fulfil individual and organisational goals.

- **Development-Oriented**

  The development of the workforce in an organisation is crucial to the nature of human resource management. HR managers use various tools to help employees understand their strengths and unleash their potential. Regular training programs can benefit employees by improving their skills. Also, monetary and non-monetary reinforcement can help people stay motivated to perform better.

- **Action Oriented**

  While human resource management does follow the rules and policies, its main focus is on action and results rather than rules. A human resource manager stresses the importance of providing effective solutions for employee problems, tensions, or controversies.

- **Forward-Looking**

  Sustaining in the competitive business environment requires organisations to plan long-term strategies. HRM is a future-oriented approach that evaluates the human resource requirements and ensures the availability of required personnel in the right place at the right time. With the forward-looking nature of human resource management, managers prepare employees by motivation, training, and development to face current and future challenges in the changing business environment.

- **Continuous Process**

  Human resource management is not a 'one-time' function. Rather, it is a never-ending process that must be performed continuously to achieve organisational objectives effectively. It involves a series of tasks, beginning with identifying the human resource requirement and continuing with recruitment, training, performance evaluation, and appraisal.

- **Basis of Other Functional Areas**

  HRM is the basis of all other functional areas of management, such as finance, production, and marketing. The effectiveness of each of these departments depends on the effectiveness of their human resource management.

- **Interdisciplinary Function**

  Human resource management is multidisciplinary in nature. HR managers utilise knowledge and inputs from various disciplines to manage the workforce effectively. The five major disciplines in HRM include management, communication, psychology, sociology, and economics. In order to effectively manage human resources, one must understand the contribution of all these disciplines to HRM.

If you want to land your dream HRM job or get a promotion, check out our post-graduate certificate course in human resource management. The course will help you understand the nature of human resource management. Moreover, you will gain the knowledge and skills needed to manage human resources effectively.

Objectives of Human Resource Management

The primary objective of human resource management is to fulfil the human capital requirements of an organisation by placing personnel in the right position at the right time. Moreover, it aims to achieve maximum employee development and contribute to realising organisational goals. The four main objectives of HRM include:-

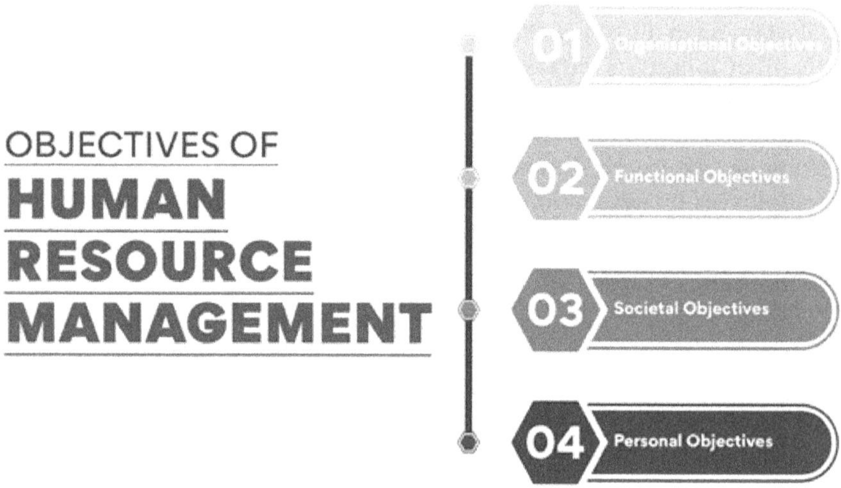

- **Organisational Objectives**

  In an organisation, HRM's objective is to maintain a competent workforce. How? By planning, recruiting, selecting, training, and developing the human resources for the organisation's growth, expansion, and survival.

  Another critical organisational objective of HRM includes facilitating other departments and helping them function smoothly. The action-oriented nature of human resource management assists an organisation in achieving its goals. As an HR manager, you should ensure the effective utilisation of human resources to help the organisation reach its goals.

- **Functional Objectives**

  Human resource management is responsible for coordination within and among different functional departments of the organisation. It organises and allocates the resources to achieve business objectives effectively.

  The objective of HRM is to provide every functional department with employees who possess the required set of skills and knowledge. To fulfil this very nature of human resource management, HR managers must ensure the timely completion of functions by the workforce. Moreover, it is important to continuously provide employees with opportunities and direct them toward the organisation's goals.

- **Societal Objectives**

  HRM is responsible for ensuring compliance with society's legal and ethical standards at every level of the organisation. The activities of HRM should be socially responsible and fulfil society's needs, demands, and challenges. Therefore, HR managers must ensure that the available resources are used for society's benefit.

  To achieve this objective, HR managers develop programs that meet employees' psychological, social, ethical, and economic needs. Some examples of these programs include equal opportunities, compensation and benefits, and community relations. By fulfiling the societal objectives of employees, HRM aims to motivate and retain productive employees.

- **Personal Objectives**

  Employees' long-term association and commitment with an organisation depend on their ability to achieve personal goals. Therefore, HRM stresses the importance of fulfilling employees' personal objectives and increasing their contribution to the organisation.

  To prevent employee performance deterioration, HR managers must help the workforce create a work-life balance. They should also be provided with adequate training and feedback on their performance. Why? Because it helps employees identify weak areas and rectify them.

Some other objectives of human resource management include the following:-

- **Foster a Better Work Culture**

  Improving employee relations is an inherent nature of human resource management. One of the most important aspects of employee relations is their work environment. Effective HRM requires developing strategies that promote a better work culture. Some examples of fostering a work culture include developing and maintaining healthy relations between team members, empowering the employees, and adopting quick on boarding processes.

- **Adopt Tools for Team Integration**

  Effective team coordination is one of the major objectives of human resource management. Higher productivity is the result of proper connections between employees in the organization. How to achieve that, you ask? By ensuring easy communication between individuals and groups at various enterprise levels! Therefore, HR managers search for tools or portals that improve data availability and make integration smooth and easier.

- **Increase Employee Engagement**

  While every department in the company can and should implement employee engagement programs, HRM is vital to successful employee engagement measures. HR managers organize events, activities, and celebrations within the organisation that not only helps in team development and employee engagement but also foster employee confidence. Moreover, boosting employee engagement can help HR managers impact employee retention, well-being, and productivity.

- **Define an Organisational Structure**

  Though important, hiring the right person for the right task is only a small part of the process. Once the employee is hired, the HR department needs to define an organisational structure to nurture employee skills. The organisational structure required for a manufacturing firm varies significantly from a hospital or an academic institution. HRM is responsible for recognising the structures and practices that would work in that specific work environment.

Now that you know the nature of human resource management and the objectives of HR managers in an organisation, let's understand the scope of HRM.

Scope of Human Resource Management

Human resource management has a wide scope. Every big and small department in an organisation needs human resources and, as a result, human resource management. The scope of HRM can be divided into three different aspects:-

- **The Personnel Aspect**

  Ensuring the individual growth of each employee is in the nature of human resource management, which can indirectly affect the organisation's overall growth. This aspect is concerned with activities like assessing human resource requirements, recruitment, selection, placement, promotion, training and development, transfer, incentives, remuneration, productivity, lay-off, retrenchment, etc.

- **The Employee Welfare Aspect**

  The objective is to ensure proper working conditions and amenities like canteens, creches, lunch rooms, restrooms, housing, transport, recreation facilities, etc., at the workplace. HRM is responsible for eliminating workplace hazards and providing employees with job safety, education, health and medical services, and more.

- **The Industrial Relation Aspect**

  The objective is to maintain peace and harmony in the organisation. How? By interacting with the labour union, addressing their grievances, and settling disputes! The aspect covers union-management relations, consultation, bargaining, grievance action, and dispute settlement.

Summing It Up!

HRM plays an integral part in the smooth running of an organisation. It is a complex process that requires HR managers to devise different solutions every time. With the evolving nature of human resource management, managers today require more patience, a mindful approach, and a diplomatic attitude to handle an organisation's human resources. More and more firms now realise the importance of hiring the right people for the right job at the right time.

Functions of HRM:

1. Job design and job analysis
2. Employee hiring and selection
3. Employee training & development
4. Compensation and Benefits
5. Employee performance management
6. Managerial relations
7. Labour relations
8. Employee engagement & communication
9. Health and safety regulations
10. Personal support for employees
11. Succession Planning
12. Industrial Relations

HRM Process includes the Followings :

1. **Recruitment:** Recruitment is one of the most signifant part of the HRM process. Recruitment process of a company depends on the human resource management which issues recruitment notifications through websites, newspapers & articles. In other words, it is a process of inviting eligible candidates to join the organization through various modes.

   Recruitments are of two types, internal & external. Internal recruitment is when the organization recruits candidates within its workforce. Whereas, external recruitment process refers when the company or organization recruits eligible candidates outside its workforce by issuing notification.

2. **Selection:** Selection is the second step of the HRM process in which, an organization selects candidates based on eligibility criteria which includes knowing particular work & having particular skill, education, attitude. All the candidates invited for recruitment may not get selected since the recruitment process includes various stages where one might get rejected. Selection process often includes two to three stages, such as preliminary interview, screening of applicants, employment tests, selection interview etc.

3. **Training:** Training comes after selection to boost the knowledge & updating the skill of the selected candidates for the requirement of particular job role. Optimizing cost & helping to maximize the efficiency of selected candidates is one of the prime roles of human resource management.The Human Resource Management Process helps to identify the training needs, preparing the training programme & implementing it & also preparing the learners.

   Job training are of two types, on the job & off the job training. On the job training is the training which is provided at the workplace & with the equipments which are at the office itself. It includes job rotation, coaching, job instruction through step by step or by assigning particular work.

   Whereas, off the job training implies where selected candidates are trained away from the actual work floor with provided equipments that are solely meant for traning purposes. Candidates are required to learn the techniques & skills in this period in order to work efficiently on the actual work floor.

4. **Assessing performance:** Assessing performance of an employee is conducted through comparing the efficiency of the present employee & the standard which has already been set previously by the organization itself. The HRM also gives feedback to the employees so that they can improve themselves as per the requirement of the organization. Whereas, performance appraisal is the to determine whether the employees will be promoted or demoted.

The employees' performance assessment can be done in two ways i.e. through traditional methods and modern methods. The example of the traditional methods are rating scale or a checklist method, where in technological advancement are not involved. Modern methods include behaviourally anchored rating scale, critical incident method, assessment centre method et cetera. The performance assessment boosts the Human Resource Management Process as a while.

5. **Motivating:** Motive is something that cause a person to act, in most cases, motivating comes under the clause when a person completes the task he will get a reward of fulfilment. The efficient Human Resource Management Proess motivates & encourages employees to reach their maximum efficiency by giving their cent percent at work.

   HRM often motivates employees to do better by giving them Rewards and Recognition & other benefits, such as different allowances & perks other than mentioned in the payslip.

   The rewards are often given in a non-financial way by giving best employees recognition for the work they have done for the company. Such as, annual or montly awards.

6. **Compensating:** Before compensating the employees for their work, the HRM needs to assess the work carefully so that it doesn't negatively impact the financial budget of the organization. The HRM process is the one segment of company which assess the gravity of compensation & manages compensation effectively, the management must be aware of the labour laws of the country in compliance with international labour organization.

7. **Maintaining Labour Relations:** Maintaining proper & healthy relationship with the employees is also a task of the HRM. The management develops the policies related to employee relations and ensures the application of company policies and procedures. They also take the responsibility of the employee-employer relationship dispute to resolve.

8. **Healthy welfare & safety of employees:** Human Resource Management Process has to ensure proper safety & healthy environment to work for the employees under law. Such as ensuring proper cleanliness, drinking water, latrines & urinals, spittoons, ventilation & temperature, disposal of waste & effluents, lighting, first aid appliances, washing, canteen, shelter, lunch room etcetera.

9. **Compliance to labor laws:** The labour laws such as mines act or minimum wages act etc. should be in accordance with the compliance. The HRM process incorporates not only the national labour laws, but also the international labour laws according to the industry as well as economic standards.

Conclusion

Lastly, we can conclude that, HRM is an important segment of a company through which new eligible workforce is recruited & trained. It also analyzes the performances of employees & provides appraisals & compensation to them. The Human Resource Management Process also ensures proper healthy & safe work environment to the workforce in compliance with labor laws. The HRM process also helps achieving maximizing efficiency of workforce by maintaining healthy employer-employee relationship. In short, we can say, it plays a crucial role in almost every aspect & contributes in the overall development of an organization.

Human Resource Manager-

The Human Resource Manager will lead and direct the routine functions of the Human Resources (HR) department including hiring and interviewing staff, administering pay, benefits, and leave, and enforcing company policies and practices.

Supervisory Responsibilities:

- Recruits, interviews, hires, and trains new staff in the department.
- Oversees the daily workflow of the department.
- Provides constructive and timely performance evaluations.
- Handles discipline and termination of employees in accordance with company policy.

Duties/Responsibilities:

- Partners with the leadership team to understand and execute the organization's human resource and talent strategy particularly as it relates to current and future talent needs, recruiting, retention, and succession planning.
- Provides support and guidance to HR generalists, management, and other staff when complex, specialized, and sensitive questions and issues arise; may be required to administer and execute routine tasks in delicate circumstances such as providing reasonable accommodations, investigating allegations of wrongdoing, and terminations.
- Manages the talent acquisition process, which may include recruitment, interviewing, and hiring of qualified job applicants, particularly for managerial, exempt, and professional roles; collaborates with departmental managers to understand skills and competencies required for openings.
- Analyzes trends in compensation and benefits; researches and proposes competitive base and incentive pay programs to ensure the organization attracts and retains top talent.

- Creates learning and development programs and initiatives that provide internal development opportunities for employees.
- Oversees employee disciplinary meetings, terminations, and investigations.
- Maintains compliance with federal, state, and local employment laws and regulations, and recommended best practices; reviews policies and practices to maintain compliance.
- Maintains knowledge of trends, best practices, regulatory changes, and new technologies in human resources, talent management, and employment law.
- Performs other duties as assigned.

Required Skills/Abilities:

- Excellent verbal and written communication skills.
- Excellent interpersonal, negotiation, and conflict resolution skills.
- Excellent organizational skills and attention to detail.
- Strong analytical and problem-solving skills.
- Ability to prioritize tasks and to delegate them when appropriate.
- Ability to act with integrity, professionalism, and confidentiality.
- Thorough knowledge of employment-related laws and regulations.
- Proficient with Microsoft Office Suite or related software.
- Proficiency with or the ability to quickly learn the organizations HRIS and talent management systems.

Education and Experience:

- Bachelor's degree in Human Resources, Business Administration, or related field required.
- A minimum of three years of human resource management experience preferred.
- SHRM-CP or SHRM-SCP highly desired.

Physical Requirements:

- Prolonged periods of sitting at a desk and working on a computer.
- Must be able to lift 15 pounds at times.
- Must be able to access and navigate each department at the organization's facilities.

Common misconceptions about HR

Five things people get wrong about HR

Over the years, I've heard many inaccurate, and often amusing, assumptions of what working in HR is like from outside perspectives. One being, "HR sounds like an easy number they just hire and fire people" Fellow HR leaders, does this sound familiar?

We take the stereotypes about HR in good humour, as all professionals do, but it's apparent that most people don't understand the value HR brings to organisations. As a senior HR professional with over 20 years of experience, I'd like to share some of my thoughts on the common misconceptions about HR and shine a light on the truth.

1. **"HR is all about helping people"**
   Without a doubt, this is the most common misconception about HR. Some people are keen to get into HR because they want to help people. While HR plays a part in looking after people in an organisation, the "looking after people" element is specifically around ensuring the organisation is set up with a robust people strategy that delivers a positive culture with engaged employees which in turn enables the business to attract and retain the very best talent in the market. When someone says they want a career in HR to help people, they are probably more suited to becoming a line manager rather than a HR professional.

2. **"HR isn't strategic"**
   On the contrary, HR leaders are required to be commercially savvy and understand the business and how to strategically manage human resources in line with their organisation's business objectives. HR can have a huge impact on the bottom line. We know that engaged employees are more productive so if HR can deliver a strong people strategy in line with the business objectives then this creates an opportunity to increase productivity.

3. **"There is a lot of paperwork in HR"**
   Leading on from my last point, many people believe that a big part of HR is filing paperwork, completing employee contracts and signing references, however, HR has evolved from an admin-heavy function into something much more strategic. Additionally, the HR function has embraced technology with open arms and many of the time-consuming manual processes that plagued HR in the past are now fully automated or completed by employees through self-service. Indeed, HR and payroll are inextricably linked which provides a 'single source of truth' of employee data to help HR leaders make strategic business decisions.

4. **"HR only exists to protect the company"**
   Some people think that HR will always take the organisation's side and that we only pay lip service to employee complaints. I've always found this to be an odd misconception, because HR bridges the gap between the

organisation and the employees. The HR team have a responsibility to act on a complaint, no matter who is involved. It may sound cheesy, but employees are at the heart of every successful organisation. I've always been very lucky to work in businesses where the business Directors have high ethical standards and would fully expect the HR team to investigate any complaints regardless of who is involved.

5. **"HR people don't know numbers"**

   Although we might not be accountants, most HR professionals have a head for numbers. As I've mentioned, the role of HR is more strategic and when it comes down to it, everything is measured by figures. HR departments live by budgets and costs, and we must demonstrate ROI for any new piece of equipment, software, like any other commercial department in the organisation.

To wrap up, the HR function is much more complex and strategic than most people assume. HR goes beyond making employees feel valued and happy at work, we take care of the organisation's wellbeing and contribute to its future growth. The value of HR is only going to increase as the workforce gets more complex.

Have you heard any other misconceptions? I'd love to hear what fellow HR professionals have heard over the years. Please feel free to share your experiences in the comments section.

Human Resource Development

Human Resource Development is the part of human resource management that specifically deals with training and development of the employees in the organization.

Human resource development includes training a person after he or she is first hired, providing opportunities to learn new skills, distributing resources that are beneficial for the employee's tasks, and any other developmental activities.

Introduction

Development of human resources is essential for any organisation that would like to be dynamic and growth-oriented. Unlike other resources, human resources have rather unlimited potential capabilities. The potential can be used only by creating a climate that can continuously identify, bring to surface, nurture and use the capabilities of people. Human Resource Development (HRD) system aims at creating such a climate. A number of HRD techniques have been developed in recent years to perform the above task based on certain principles. This unit provides an understanding of the concept of HRD system, related mechanisms and the changing boundaries of HRD.

HRD concept was first introduced by Leonard Nadler in 1969 in a conference in US. *"He defined HRD as those learning experience which are organized, for a specific time, and designed to bring about the possibility of behavioral change"*.

Human Resource Development (HRD) is the framework for helping employees develop their personal and organizational skills, knowledge, and abilities. Human Resource Development includes such opportunities as employee training, employee career development, performance management and development, coaching, mentoring, succession planning, key employee identification, tuition assistance, and organization development. The focus of all aspects of Human Resource Development is on developing the most superior workforce so that the organization and individual employees can accomplish their work goals in service to customers.

Human Resource Development can be formal such as in classroom training, a college course, or an organizational planned change effort. Or, Human Resource Development can be informal as in employee coaching by experts in the industry or by a manager. Healthy organizations believe in Human Resource Development and cover all of these bases.

Definitions of HRD

HRD (Human Resources Development) has been defined by various scholars in various ways. Some of the important definitions of HRD (Human Resources Development) are as follows:

- According to Leonard Nadler, "Human resource development is a series of organised activities, conducted within a specialised time and designed to produce behavioural changes."
- In the words of Prof. T.V. Rao, "HRD is a process by which the employees of an organisation are helped in a continuous and planned way to (i) acquire or sharpen capabilities required to perform various functions associated with their present or expected future roles; (ii) develop their general capabilities as individual and discover and exploit their own inner potential for their own and /or organisational development purposes; (iii) develop an organisational culture in which superior-subordinate relationship, team work and collaboration among sub-units are strong and contribute to the professional well being, motivation and pride of employees." .
- According to M.M. Khan, "Human resource development is the across of increasing knowledge, capabilities and positive work attitudes of all people working at all levels in a business undertaking."

The Concept of Human Resource Development

Human resource development in the organisation context is a process by which the employees of an organisation are helped, in a continuous and planned way to:

1. Acquire or sharpen capabilities required to perform various functions associated with their present or expected future roles;
2. Develop their general capabilities as individuals and discover and exploit their own inner potentials for their own and/or organisational development purposes; and
3. Develop an organisational culture in which supervisor-subordinate relationships, teamwork and collaboration among sub-units are strong and contribute to the professional well being, motivation and pride of employees.

This definition of HRD is limited to the organisational context. In the context of a state or nation it would differ.

HRD is a process, not merely a set of mechanisms and techniques. The mechanisms and techniques such as performance appraisal, counselling, training, and organization development interventions are used to initiate, facilitate, and promote this process in a continuous way. Because the process has no limit, the mechanisms may need to be examined periodically to see whether they are promoting or hindering the process. Organisations can facilitate this process of development by planning for it, by allocating organisational resources for the purpose, and by exemplifying an HRD philosophy that values human beings and promotes their development.

Difference between HRD and HRM

Both are very important concepts of management specifically related with human resources of organisation. Human resource management and human resource development can be differentiated on the following grounds:

- The human resource management is mainly maintenance oriented whereas human resource development is development oriented.
- Organisation structure in case of human resources management is independent whereas human resource development creates a structure, which is inter-dependent and inter-related.
- Human resource management mainly aims to improve the efficiency of the employees whereas aims at the development of the employees as well as organisation as a whole.
- Responsibility of human resource development is given to the personnel/ human resource management department and specifically to personnel manager whereas responsibility of HRD is given to all managers at various levels of the organisation.
- HRM motivates the employees by giving them monetary incentives or rewards whereas human resource development stresses on motivating people by satisfying higher-order needs.

Basis of Differentiation	HRM	HRD
Definition and full form	The full form of HRM is Human Resource Management. It refers to how the principles of management can be applied to manage the employees working in an organization effectively.	The full form of HRD is Human Resource Development. It refers to continuous development functions that are implemented for improving the performance of those working in an organization.
Nature	HRM is a management function.	HRD is a sub-function of HRM.
Function	The functions of HRM are reactive and are usually applied to gaining holistic organizational goals.	The functions of HRD are proactive and have to be applied consistently to enhance the productivity of employees.
Goal	The objective of HRM is related to improving the overall performance of employees.	HRD goals are usually connected with skill development, knowledge enhancement, and increasing the competency of employees.
Process	Most HRM processes are routine and have to be carried out as and when the need arises.	HRD processes are ongoing and not occasional.
Dependency	HRM is an independent entity in itself. It comprises of different sections inclusive of recruitment and retention, HRD, compensation, performance, appraisal management, etc.	HRD is a subsystem of HRM and draws many functions, attributes, and processes from HRM.
Concerned with	HRM deals with and has concerns for people only. It handles recruitment, rewards, etc.	HRD is concerned with the development of all aspects and people within an organization and manages its skill development processes.
Levels of formality	HRM functions are generally formal and are applied via classroom/laboratory training, etc.	HRD functions may be informal as in mentorships, employees receive coaching from superiors, usually managers.

The Need for HRD

HRD is needed by any organisation that wants to be dynamic and growth-oriented or to succeed in a fast-changing environment. Organisations can become dynamic and grow only through the efforts and competencies of their human resources. Personnel policies can keep the morale and motivation of employees high, but these efforts are not enough to make the organisation dynamic and take it in new directions. Employee capabilities must continuously be acquired, sharpened, and used. For this purpose, an "enabling" organisational culture is essential. When employees use their initiative, take risks, experiment, innovate, and make things happen, the organisation may be said to have an "enabling" culture.

Even an organisation that has reached its limit of growth, needs to adapt to the changing environment. No organisation is immune to the need for processes that help to acquire and increase its capabilities for stability and renewal.

HRD Functions

The core of the concept of HRS is that of development of human beings, or HRD. The concept of development should cover not only the individual but also other units in the organisation. In addition to developing the individual, attention needs to be given to the development of stronger dyads, i.e., two-person groups of the employee and his boss. Such dyads are the basic units of working in the organisation. Besides several groups like committees, task groups, etc. also require attention. Development of such groups should be from the point of view of increasing collaboration amongst people working in the organisation, thus making for an effective decision-making. Finally, the entire department and the entire organisation also should be covered by development. Their development would involve developing a climate conducive for their effectiveness, developing self-renewing mechanisms in the organisations so that they are able to adjust and pro-act, and developing relevant processes which contribute to their effectiveness. Hence, the goals of the HRD systems are to develop:

1. The capabilities of each employee as an individual.
2. The capabilities of each individual in relation to his or her present role.
3. The capabilities of each employee in relation to his or her expected future role(s).
4. The dyadic relationship between each employee and his or her supervisor.
5. The team spirit and functioning in every organisational unit (department, group, etc.).
6. Collaboration among different units of the organisation.
7. The organisation's overall health and self-renewing capabilities which, in turn, increase the enabling capabilities of individuals, dyads, teams, and the entire organisation.

Features of Human Resource development

The essential features of human resource development can be listed as follows:

- Human resource development is a process in which employees of the organisations are recognized as its human resource. It believes that human resource is most valuable asset of the organisation.
- It stresses on development of human resources of the organisation. It helps the employees of the organisation to develop their general capabilities in relation to their present jobs and expected future role.
- It emphasise on the development and best utilization of the capabilities of individuals in the interest of the employees and organisation.
- It helps is establishing/ developing better inter-personal relations. It stresses on developing relationship based on help, trust and confidence.
- It promotes team spirit among employees.
- It tries to develop competencies at the organisation level. It stresses on providing healthy climate for development in the organisation.
- HRD is a system. It has several sub-systems. All these sub-systems are inter-related and interwoven. It stresses on collaboration among all the sub-systems.
- It aims to develop an organisational culture in which there is good senior-subordinate relations, motivation, quality and sense of belonging.
- It tries to develop competence at individual, inter-personal, group and organisational level to meet organisational goal.
- It is an inter-disciplinary concept. It is based on the concepts, ideas and principles of sociology, psychology, economics etc.
- It form on employee welfare and quality of work life. It tries to examine/ identify employee needs and meeting them to the best possible extent.
- It is a continuous and systematic learning process. Development is a life long process, which never ends.

Benefits of Human Resource Development

Human resource development now a days is considered as the key to higher productivity, better relations and greater profitability for any organisation. Appropriate HRD provides unlimited benefits to the concerned organisation. Some of the important benefits are being given here:

- HRD (Human Resource Development) makes people more competent. HRD develops new skill, knowledge and attitude of the people in the concern organisations.
- With appropriate HRD programme, people become more committed to their jobs. People are assessed on the basis of their performance by having

a acceptable performance appraisal system.

- An environment of trust and respect can be created with the help of human resource development.
- Acceptability toward change can be created with the help of HRD. Employees found themselves better equipped with problem-solving capabilities.
- It improves the all round growth of the employees. HRD also improves team spirit in the organisation. They become more open in their behaviour. Thus, new values can be generated.
- It also helps to create the efficiency culture In the organisation. It leads to greater organisational effectiveness. Resources are properly utilised and goals are achieved in a better way.
- It improves the participation of worker in the organisation. This improve the role of worker and workers feel a sense of pride and achievement while performing their jobs.
- It also helps to collect useful and objective data on employees programmes and policies which further facilitate better human resource planning.
- Hence, it can be concluded that HRD provides a lot of benefits in every organisation. So, the importance of concept of HRD should be recognised and given a place of eminence, to face the present and future challenges in the organisation.

Colour coding HRD, Samsung style

It could well be a resort. It is, though in a different sort of way. The complex, located on rolling hills an hour's drive from Seoul, is Samsung's Human Resources Development (HRD) Centre, the place where the South Korean giant forges the mind and heart of its employees to its philosophy. Samsung takes its people seriously. It is constantly preparing them, at every level, for the rapidly changing world market that throws up ever-changing challenges. Employees of all the 70-plus companies of the group at one time or the other come here to be inspired and to learn to think out of the box..

Indeed, so serious is Samsung about its people thinking differently and spontaneously that it has designed the campus unlike any other. While many training/excellence centers recreate the college campus, Samsung has ideated differently, colour-coding its values and integrating them all over the campus so that these values get hard-wired among the trainees. If for people, it is Purple, it is Blue for Excellence, Red for Change, Green for Integrity and Orange for Co-prosperity.

But the predominant theme in the campus is Green, emphasizing the company's commitment to integrity. As Mr Ja Hwan Song, Vice-President, Globalization Team, HRD Centre, recently told a group journalists from India, the people philosophy is quite simply giving them a wealth of opportunities to reach their full potential. Realizing that change is a constant and the innovation is critical to keep pace, the HRD Centre tries to equip its people to think differently.

Believing that a business cannot be successful unless it creates prosperity and opportunity for others, he says Samsung cares as much for its staff as for societies it operates in by being socially and environmentally responsible.

The training center prepares new comers to Samsung for the journey with the organization, promotes to take up the new responsibilities, senior executives to exchange ideas, and the top echelons to think far into the future. This is done chiefly through three key initiatives:

Shared Value Program: The attempt is to give new comers the basics of doing good business. History, tradition, values form the basis of the program with sessions on teamwork and creativity.

Business Leader Program: A five-month initiative to develop the leaders of the next generation.

The participants are those with global competitiveness and all-round management skills. Global business management, leadership, and problem solving are the focus.

Structure of Human Resource Devlopment-

Chart 2 *Organizational Chart for Integrated HRD*

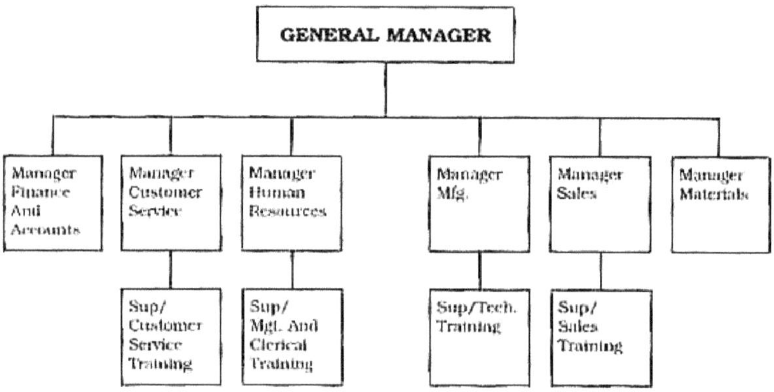

Chart 3 *Organizational Chart for HRD as a Separate Department*

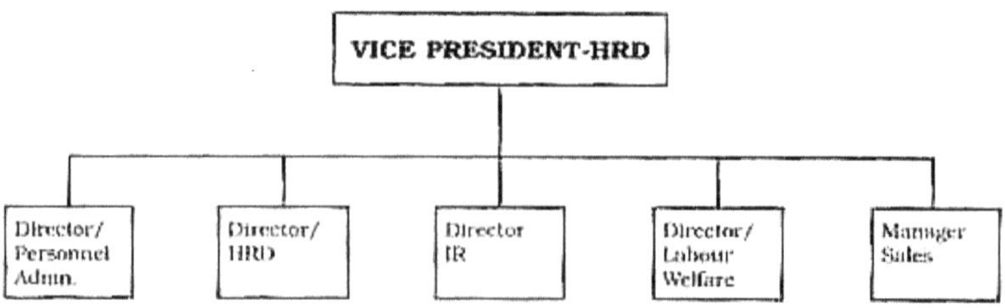

Role of Human Resource Manager-

The Human Resource Manager will lead and direct the routine functions of the Human Resources (HR) department including hiring and interviewing staff, administering pay, benefits, and leave, and enforcing company policies and practices.

Main Roles of HRD Manager-

From the foregoing discussions, it is apparent that the primary goal of HRD is to increase worker's productivity and firm's profitability as investment in HRD improves worker's skill and enhance motivation. The other goal of HRD is to prevent obsolescence at all levels. To achieve these two goals, HRD Manager of any organization plays following two important roles:

1. To assist people in obtaining the knowledge and skills they need for present and future jobs and to assist them in attaining their personal goals.
2. To play the 'enabling' role, providing the right context in which human performance occurs and the organization reaches its stated objectives.

Advertisements:

In 1998, ASTD identified eleven roles of HRD manager, which can be enumerated as follows:

1. **Administrator:**

   The role of providing coordination and support services for the delivery of HRD programmes and services.

2. **Evaluator:**

   The role of identifying the impact of an intervention on individual or organizational effectiveness.

3. **Individual Career Development Advisor:**

   The role of helping individuals to assess personal competencies, values and goals and to identify, plan and implement development and career actions.

4. **HRD Manager:**

   The role of supporting and leading a group's work and linking that work with total organization.

5. **Instructor/Facilitator:**

   The role of presenting information, directing structured learning experiences and managing group discussions and group process.

6. **Marketer:**

   The role of marketing and contracting from HRD's viewpoints, programmes and services.

7. **Material Developer:**

   The role of producing written and/or electronically mediated instructional materials.

8. **Needs Analyst:**

   The role of identifying ideal and actual performance and performance conditions and determining causes of discrepancies.

9. **Organizational Change:**

   The role of influencing and supporting changes in organizational behaviour.

10. **Programme Designer:**

    The role of preparing objectives, defining content and selecting and sequencing activities for a specific intervention.

11. **Researcher:**

    The role of identifying, developing or testing new information (theory, concepts, technology, models, hardware) and translating these two implications for improved individual or organizational performance.

Top Factors Affecting Human Resource

Human Resource Management is the most significant aspect of any enterprise because it involves effective management of the employees in the organisation. Employees are the biggest assets of any organisation, which makes Human Resource Management a domain that needs to be highly effective in order to make the employees as well as the organisation strive towards success.

However, Human Resource Management is more complex than one can imagine, because of the large diversity of the employees that results in people from different backgrounds working together. It is because of the complexity of Human Resource Management that the HR department is one of the key departments in any organisation. A new age human resources software like Digital HRMS is designed to help the HR department take the right steps towards successful Human Resource Management. So, it makes one wonder about what exactly makes Human Resource Management successful. Let us take a closer look.

1] **Implementation of Technology**

   Implementation of HR Technology is one of the biggest factors affecting human resource management in an organisation. This is because today you have advanced HR software platforms that are designed to automate every aspect of HR functions. This results in a boost in HR productivity and efficiency, along with more effective employee management.

2] **The Work Environment**

It was until last year that the conventional office environment was the only thing people would imagine. However, Covid-19 pandemic changed it all for good and today we are slowly getting used to the current situation where most of us are working from home. This new situation has brought forth its own share of challenges for the employees as well as for the HR in terms of human resource management.

3] **Availability of Good Talent**

Are expert professionals readily available for hiring? Sometimes, that's not the case and a situation like this can be stressful for the human resource management department, because it becomes increasingly difficult to find the right resources for open positions in the organisation. This can result in positions remaining open for extended period of time or the organisation having to compromise with resources that are not the best fit for the positions.

4] **Training and Development**

Training and development programs for the employees can be a great way to boost employee engagement and at the same time, help the organisation find resources with the exact skillset required for different positions. In other words, it can prove to be a win-win solution for the employer as well as the employees. Digital HRMS is the new age HR software platform that enables HR department to plan and manage training sessions for employees, even in times of remote work.

Importance of Human Resource Development

- **Develops Competent Workforce:** Human resource development helps in developing a superior workforce for the organization by educating and training them. It imparts all knowledge and skills to employees necessary for carrying out their roles and duties.
- **Improve Relations with Employees:** Human resource development develops a better understanding among employers and employees. Employers guides and cooperates its workforce in performing their roles. It leads to better trust and respect among them which strengthens their relations with one another.
- **Provides Opportunity for Career Development:** It works towards developing the career of all peoples working in an organization. Employees are personally provided various training and development opportunities as per their requirements. It improves people's knowledge, skills, talent, creative abilities, values and beliefs from time to time according to changing demands.

- **Enhance Productivity:** Human resources development has an effective role in increasing organizational productivity. It imparts abilities and skills to employees which are necessary for performing organizational activities. All people working are able to perform well and contribute more to an organization which enhances the overall productivity.
- **Improves Job Satisfaction:** Human resource development focuses on inspiring people for performing better. It works on the good orientation of employees and provides them with a better atmosphere for working. All this leads to high commitment towards roles among employees and results in job satisfaction.
- **Clarify the Roles:** It develops a proper communication network between employers and employees. Employers are able to explain clearly all roles and duties to their workforce. Employees can easily clarify all their doubts or problems with their superiors.

Functions of Human Resource Development

- **Training and Development:** This concept aims at improving the skills, abilities, and knowledge of people at work by training and educating them. As soon as a person joins organization several activities like orientation, skill training, counselling and coaching starts. These are meant for training and developing the employees as per organizational needs.
- **Career Development:** Career planning and development is another important function of human resource development. It is a continuous process whereby the individual improves and develops his skills. Career development comprises of two processes: career planning and career management. Career planning means the activities that employees need to perform. Whereas, career management means steps that employees need to follow to achieve the plans.
- **Performance Appraisal:** The human resource development concept aims at providing rewards and promotions to employees on the basis of their performance. It keeps a check on the performance of employees and ensures whether it is at an acceptable level.
- **Employee's Participation in Management:** Participation of peoples working in organization in decision-making is a must for better understanding and exchange of ideas. Human resource development managers work on encouraging employees to participate in organizational management. It provides a platform for mutual learning and development.
- **Improves the Working Environment:** Human resource development aims at providing a better atmosphere for people working in an organization. It ensures that all employees get fair remunerations, proper working hours and various other welfare services.

- **Organizational Change and Development:** It facilitates organizational change and development as per the requirements. It diagnosis process, structure and task force of organizations from time to time and accordingly design all training and development programs.

Unit II

HUMAN RESOURCES (HR) POLICY

Human resources policies are guidelines for hiring, work processes, compensation, leave, training, promotion, work environments, termination and other important functions. HR policies also outline how an organization will treat its people and property.

20 Must-Have HR Policies for Your Employee Handbook

HR policies are a must-have for any organization. They can guide employees and leaders about what's expected of them, ensure everyone is treated consistently, as well as prevent problems – including legal concerns.

Human Resources (HR) Policy-

Human resources policies are guidelines for hiring, work processes, compensation, leave, training, promotion, work environments, termination and other important functions. HR policies also outline how an organization will treat its people and property. They're developed by HR managers with the help of company management. It's important to enumerate the policies before issues arise so you know how to respond.

Function of HR policies-

What are HR policies? The point of HR policies is to provide a framework for an organization so leaders can make consistent decisions and ensure people are treated equitably. Implementing effective HR policies can demonstrate that you're able to meet ethical, diversity and training requirements. HR policies also help your company adhere to corporate governance and regulation of employees.

You want your company to run as smoothly and efficiently as possible and stay compliant with HR laws. HR policies add structure and provide consistency in employment and workforce matters.

Examples include:

- Ensuring fair and adequate compensation for all employees.

- Addressing employee grievances and problems and appropriate ways to address them.
- Training employees so their skills meet organizational needs.
- Providing the framework to address personnel issues.

Key Elements for HR Policies-

Although the specifics of each organization's HR policies may differ, they should all be derived from employment best practices and regulations. HR policies should be transparent and universally applied to all employees. Key elements include purpose, procedures, who needs to follow the guidelines, as well as any definitions of terms used.

Other important elements include:

- Guidelines for supervisors and managers
- Organizational goals and values
- Systems to regularly review changes that may affect employees
- Context for various programs and benefits, such as professional development and on boarding programs
- Clear steps to implement policies

HR policies are just one component of your overall workforce plan and HR strategy for employee management. So what are HR strategies and policies? The HR strategy is your overall goal for how to manage your workforce and help them grow while also boosting company performance. And the policy is how to implement that strategy. Your policies should be kept in your employee handbook and stored for easy access for employees, managers and your HR team. A human resource management system (HRMS) can help not only store the appropriate policies and procedures, but also implement some of them. For example, an HRMS can automate time off and scheduling functions.

Advantages of HR Policies-

Creating and implementing HR policies can reduce liability. Since they're meant to ensure employee-related practices are consistent and fair across the organization, well-written policies will offer leaders guidance based on compliance requirements. For instance, HR policies should help managers fairly interpret company guidelines and apply uniform treatment to all employees, regardless of age, gender, race or sexual orientation. If issues do occur, there will be policies in place to address the concerns.

By clearly listing policies, when problems do occur, you're able to act promptly and save time by not repeatedly analyzing ways to solve similar issues. Additionally, you may be legally required to communicate some of this information. And formalizing a policy and then helping employees understand where to find things like the leave policy makes navigating requests like time off easier for the employer and employee.

Plainly listing policies encourages employee engagement and helps them better understand how to navigate key moments in their career growth, such as onboarding, promotions and offboarding. Specific policies may vary by industry. But whether you're working in retail, manufacturing or the restaurant business, employee engagement and retention is vital, and HR policies help lay the groundwork for success.

HR Policies & Compliance-

HR policies need to be compliant with local, state and federal regulations, especially for companies with at least 50 employees. Even if your company has fewer than 50 workers, HR policies can help your organization be proactive about shaping company culture and encourage efficiency.

Federal & State Laws Compliance

Your HR department should make sure your company follows federal employment regulations, such as the Family Medical Leave Act (FMLA), EEO-1 reporting for federal contracts and employer-shared responsibility as it pertains to the Affordable Care Act (ACA).

City & County Laws Compliance

Organizations also need to maintain compliance with local and state regulations. For example, there may be local minimum wage laws or anti-bias rules you should be aware of when crafting your HR policies.

Top 20 HR Policies for Employee Handbooks

Along with local, state and federal policies, you also need to address factors that are relevant to the type and size of your company, as well as how to communicate the guidelines in a transparent manner. It is also important to have a process to record an employee's acknowledgement and understanding of your HR policies. Here are 20 policies to consider for your employee handbook that follow some of those policies, along with commonly accepted and best business practices.

1. **Recruiting and Hiring Policies**

   Pre-hire policies include forms like new position requisition forms, referrals and evaluation forms. Formalize the onboarding process, which includes tax forms like the W-4. Consider standardizing the interviewing, selection and contract or offer letter processes.

2. **At-Will Employment**

   State at the beginning of the employee handbook if employees are at-will, which means either the employee or the employer can end the employment at any time, as long as the reason is lawful. Check local and state regulations for at-will employment guidelines.

3. **Conduct Policies**

   The goal of employee conduct policies is to keep the workplace environment safe and comfortable for all. These include sexual harassment, alcohol and anti-discrimination policies.

4. **Employment Classification**

   Common classifications include full time, part time, exempt and non-exempt employees. These classifications help dictate eligibility for employee benefits and overtime pay.

5. **Non-Discrimination and Anti-Harassment**

   Carefully craft your non-discrimination and anti-harassment policies with review of local, state and federal laws, as the regulations may change depending on location. Include the processes to follow if issues should arise along with what constitutes harassment and discrimination.

6. **Safety Policies**

   Help employees understand safety and emergency procedures. It's important that any work-related injury is reported quickly, so share with employees how to report workplace accidents. Look for industry-specific safety policies you may need to implement to comply with regulations under the Occupational Safety and Health Act. For example, the use of heavy machinery or hazardous chemicals.

7. **Reasonable Accommodation**

   If employees with disabilities or sincerely held religious beliefs request it, you may be legally required to provide reasonable accommodation. State and federal laws may apply, so be sure to understand what's legally required and then document and communicate the policies on how employees can submit requests and what accommodation will be made. Even if employees don't submit the request in writing, be sure to document each request and any action taken.

8. **Disciplinary Termination Policies**

   These can span different types of policies, such as rules for attendance and anti-harassment, and need to cover reasons for disciplinary action that may result in termination. These policies should also include how disciplinary actions will escalate, such as going from verbal to written warnings.

9. **Compensation Policies**

   Compensation policies should cover employee benefits and payroll frequency. It should also include how employees are paid (i.e., direct deposit) and any secondary benefits, such as education reimbursements.

10. **Workplace Attire Policies**

    Appropriate workplace attire should be described in detail. Instead of using generic language like "professional attire," be specific. And include information about different environments in your workplace. For instance, if you have a lab, include what type of safety goggles need to be worn for compliance reasons, or what attire teachers can wear on sports day.

11. **Attendance Policies**

    Clearly outline for employees when they are expected to be at work and what to do if they have an unscheduled or scheduled absence or are late for work. Don't forget to include how to record time worked and break policies.

12. **Referral Program Policies**

    If you have a referral policy, include it in your employee handbook. List how any referral rewards are provided and any stipulations, like if the new hire has to stay employed for a specific time frame before the reward is given.

13. **Expense Policies**

    If you reimburse for expenses, outline what is reimbursable, the maximum amount and the procedures to request reimbursement.

14. **Leave Policies**

    Share with employees how to request time off. And list policies for sick leave, vacation time, maternity and paternity leave, and any company-recognized holidays.

15. **Sexual Harassment**

    Sexual harassment needs to be taken seriously. Keep your policies up to date and clearly communicate zero-tolerance guidelines as it relates to any inappropriate or unwelcome sexual actions or comments.

16. **Bereavement Policies**

    Bereavement policies can be included in your general leave policy section or as a separate entry for compassionate leave. Detail the time off provided and how to make a request, including what to do if employees need to take a longer leave of absence.

17. **Local and State Laws**

    Employment law will vary by location. Understand what your local and state laws require and include any variation in your employee handbook. For example, there may be differing wage and overtime laws, leave requirements or record keeping regulations.

18. **Meals and Break Periods**

    Be clear about any meal and break period rules, including how long they can last and how many breaks employees can take. Some breaks may be required, but even if it's not a legal requirement, listing your break policy is a best practice.

19. **Using Company Property**

    Include documentation and procedures for the process of using company property such as equipment or tools. Incorporate things like the condition equipment should be in when returned, as well consequences if items are either damaged or not returned.

20. **Resignation or Exit Policies**

    Make clear how employees should leave the company when they are ready to exit. Include information on how to hand in their resignation, the desired notice time and exit interview policies. Also, list reasons for involuntary termination.

Trending HR Policies

Current events and changes in the business landscape mean HR policies are not static. Addressing workplace trends can help you stay on top of best practices and protect your organization in a dynamic environment. Policies will change as your business develops, and they should support your overall human capital management efforts to help your employees grow in their careers while keeping your business nimble and adaptive.

What are the most important HR policies? Well, that will change based on your company, the location, the industry, the size and what most helps your employees. There are many that are legally mandated, and some policies are simply common and standard to include. Regardless, it's important to adjust as business situations alter.

Consider including these six trending HR policies in your employee handbook:

- **Social media policy:** Creating and enforcing social media policies can protect the reputation of your company. You may need policies for company accounts, as well as policies for your employees' personal social media profiles. Include what disciplinary measures will be taken for policy violations.
- **Remote work policy:** As workforces become increasingly mobile, help your employees understand what you expect of them. Include which employees are eligible for remote work, what limitations there are and how you'll be monitoring their work.
- **Weapons in the workplace policy (or zero tolerance for workplace violence):** Organizations should address additional violence policies, such as weapons, what items are considered weapons and behavior that's prohibited, and any disciplinary measures that will be taken for policy violations.

- **Updated confidentiality policy:** Be specific about which work-related items are confidential. Don't include items such as compensation and working conditions because those aren't considered private.
- **Drug and alcohol policy:** Expanding laws regarding the legalization of marijuana in some areas means organizations need to address how usage is addressed in the workplace. Keep in mind all local, state and federal laws regarding substance use when drafting the policy.
- **Bring your own device (BYOD) policy:** If employees use personal devices for work reasons, draft policies for privacy and security measures, as well as any monitoring that needs to occur.

Top 8 Essential Characteristics of a Sound Human Resource Policy

HR policies should possess the following characteristics:

1. The HR policy should present the principle that will guide the organisation's actions and reflect a faith in the ethical values of employees.

   As Peter Ducker has observed, "The policies of an enterprise have to be balanced with the kind of reputation an enterprise wants to build up with special reference to the social and human needs, objectives and values".

   It should be consistent with the overall philosophy and objectives of the organization, as well as with labor laws and public policy.

2 The HR policy should be formulated after considering the long range plans and needs of the organization.

   The policy should be definite, positive, clear and easily understood by everyone in the organisation so that what it proposes to achieve in the long term is evident. Only a clear policy statement can serve as a guide to thinking and decision-making.

3. The HR policy must be reasonably stable but not rigid. It should be flexible to cover a normal range of activities. Change in a policy should be made only when it is essential and at fairly long intervals.

4. The HR policy should be formulated with due regard for the interests of all the concerned parties – the employers, the employees and the public community.

   It should be stated in the broadest possible terms so as to serve as a guide in practice now and in the future.

5. The HR policy must be developed with the active participation and support of the management and the co-operation of employees at the shop floor level and in the office. It should be formulated with active participation of the trade unions as well.

6. The HR policy should be definite so that it is easy to understand. It should be stated in clear, definite and easily understood terms so that what it proposes to achieve is evident.
7. The HR policy must provide a two-way communication system between the man¬agement and the employees. It should be communicated in writing so as to re¬move any confusion. This is necessary to prevent misunderstanding and to en¬sure uniformity of application.
8. The HR policy should be consistent with public policy. A good HR policy should recognise individual differences and respect human dignity. It should be based on consistency in treatment to all employees without any favouritism or discrimination.

Scope of HR Policies-

The scope of HRM is extensive and far-reaching. Therefore, it is very difficult to define it concisely. However, we may classify the same under following heads:

1. **HRM in Personnel Management:** This is typically direct manpower management that involves manpower planning, hiring (recruitment and selection), training and development, induction and orientation, transfer, promotion, compensation, layoff and retrenchment, employee productivity.

   The overall objective here is to ascertain individual growth, development and effectiveness which indirectly contribute to organizational development.

   It also includes performance appraisal, developing new skills, disbursement of wages, incentives, allowances, traveling policies and procedures and other related courses of actions.

2. **HRM in Employee Welfare:** This particular aspect of HRM deals with working conditions and amenities at workplace. This includes a wide array of responsibilities and services such as safety services, health services, welfare funds, social security and medical services.

   It also covers appointment of safety officers, making the environment worth working, eliminating workplace hazards, support by top management, job safety, safeguarding machinery, cleanliness, proper ventilation and lighting, sanitation, medical care, sickness benefits, employment injury benefits, personal injury benefits, maternity benefits, unemployment benefits and family benefits.

   It also relates to supervision, employee counseling, establishing harmonious relationships with employees, education and training. Employee welfare is about determining employees' real needs and fulfilling them with active participation of both management and employees.

In addition to this, it also takes care of canteen facilities, creches, rest and lunch rooms, housing, transport, medical assistance, education, health and safety, recreation facilities, etc.

3. **HRM in Industrial Relations:** Since it is a highly sensitive area, it needs careful interactions with labor or employee unions, addressing their grievances and settling the disputes effectively in order to maintain peace and harmony in the organization.

   It is the art and science of understanding the employment (union-management) relations, joint consultation, disciplinary procedures, solving problems with mutual efforts, understanding human behavior and maintaining work relations, collective bargaining and settlement of disputes.

The main aim is to safeguarding the interest of employees by securing the highest level of understanding to the extent that does not leave a negative impact on organization.

It is about establishing, growing and promoting industrial democracy to safeguard the interests of both employees and management.

Formulation of HR Personnel Policy - Policy formulation and implementation involve the following steps:

1. **Identifying the need:** Initially, important areas of personnel management in HR (recruitment, selection, training compensating bargaining) must have a policy formulation that is clearly spelt out. Additional policy guidelines can come at any stage depending on the recurrence of the ticklish issues at various levels.

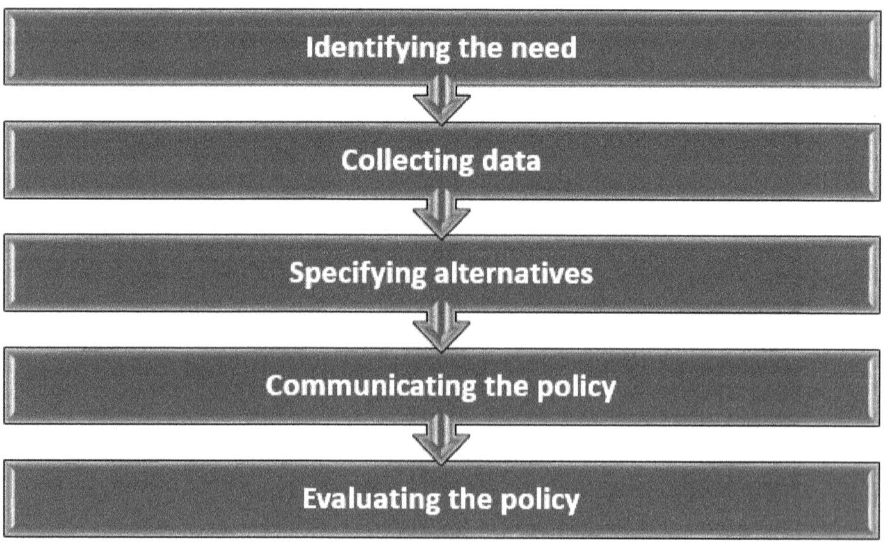

2. **Collecting data:** Once priority areas are listed, steps should be taken to collect facts before formulating a policy. Various sources could be tapped for these purposes such as (1) company's records (2) past practices (3) survey of industry practices (4) experience of personnel handling various issues (5) top management philosophy (6) organizational culture (7) employee aspirations and (8) changing economic, social an legislative environment, etc.
3. **Specifying alternatives:** Policy alternatives should emerge clearly after collecting relevant data from various sources. These have to be evaluated carefully in terms of their contribution to organizational objectives. It is always better to involve people at various levels, especially those who are going to use and live with such policies. Top management should put the stamp of approval only when everything is above board and the stated policy clearly reflects organizational priorities.
4. **Communicating the policy:** In order to gain approval at various levels, the formulated policy should be communicated throughout the organization. Policy manuals, in-house journals, and discussions with people at various levels may be used to reach out to employees quickly.
5. **Evaluating the policy:** Personnel policies, to be effective must be reviewed evaluated and controlled regularly against certain established standards. Evaluation helps determine changes in existing policies. All these policies should be reviewed annually and some policies should be reviewed at specific times for example when there is collective bargaining or after strike / lock out etc. Departmental policies may be reviewed through the participation of all employees. Outside consultants or experts from other organizations may be engaged to review crucial policies. Adequate care should be taken to review the policies in the following situations when (1) employees offer suggestions ; (2) employees express grievances (3) unsatisfactory reports about employees performance and behavior (4) company plans for change like expansion, diversification, contraction, adoption of new technology and introduction of new methods. Personnel policies, to be effective should have a favorable impact on the objectives and functions of P /HRM and help the parties concerned.

Need for Formulation of Personnel Policy

Formulating a personnel policy is necessary for several reasons. These include:

1. **Setting clear expectations:** A personnel policy establishes clear guidelines and expectations for employee behavior, conduct, and performance. This helps to ensure consistency in the workplace and provides a framework for addressing issues and concerns.
2. **Compliance with laws and regulations:** A personnel policy ensures that the organization complies with relevant employment laws and regulations,

such as those related to discrimination, equal employment opportunity, and workplace safety.

3. **Attracting and retaining employees:** An organization that has a well-formulated personnel policy can attract and retain employees by providing a clear and fair framework for compensation, benefits, and performance management.
4. **Promoting a positive work environment:** A personnel policy can promote a positive work environment by setting expectations for respectful behavior, addressing harassment and discrimination, and promoting work-life balance.
5. **Enhancing organizational performance:** A personnel policy that is aligned with organizational goals and values can enhance organizational performance by promoting employee engagement, productivity, and commitment to the organization.

Types of HR Policies:

Company HR policies and procedures are very important in any organization. They must be regularized among the employees of the organization, so as to avoid all the uncertain issues that might arise.

The initial responsibility of any employee will be to get synced with the work culture of the organization, in such a case HR policies help them give an idea about the do's and don'ts one must follow. Some of the top human resource policies are,

- Attendance
- Behavior
- Requests
- Safety

Top Factors Affecting Human Resource Management

- 1] Implementation of Technology.
- 2] The Work Environment.
- 3] Availability of Good Talent.
- 4] Training and Development.

The core HR processes include:

- Human resource planning.
- Recruitment.
- Selection.
- Hiring.

- On boarding.
- Training.
- Employee relations.
- Performance appraisals.

Human Resource Policies and Procedures-

The scope of the human resource department has changed over the years, as it has become an important part of the strategic planning processes of an organization. Human resource professionals aid in creating policies and procedures for the organization that cover areas such as training and development, recruiting, and disciplinary measures. The department is also responsible for employee relations, compensation and benefits, and compliance with federal and state employment laws.

HR policies and procedures provide written guidelines that the organization and its employees must comply with. They also help management with the day-to-day interactions with employees by ensuring that each employee is being treated fairly and that the company is being consistent in its actions.

Purpose of HR Policies and Procedures

The human resource department must institute policies and procedures that are beneficial to the organization, protect the employees, and are compliant with the law. They also help protect the organization from legal claims. The government is responsible for determining if an organization is complying with employment law, usually in the form of government mandates. A government mandate is a law that organizations must follow to ensure that they are treating their employees fairly and that safety measures are being followed.

There are several agencies that the government has in place that hold companies responsible for following employment law. One of these government agencies is the Equal Employment Opportunity Commission. This agency was established in 1964 to ensure that companies with 15 or more employees are complying with Title VII of the Civil Rights Act.

Another agency that aids in enforcing government mandates is the United States Department of Labor. It administers federal law and guarantees that workers have a healthy, fair, and safe work environment. It covers minimum wage, unemployment insurance, discrimination protection, etc. Each state also has its own labor department that institutes its state labor laws.

Importance of HR Guidelines

HR guidelines are very important to an organization. The policies and procedures instituted by the HR department help the organization to provide protection, ensure government compliance, and provide guidance. There are several other reasons why having clear guidelines in the organization is important::

- They give the employees a clear picture of what is expected of them, the benefits that are available through the organization, and their rights.
- They codify the organization's commitment to following any applicable federal and state laws and regulations.
- They provide guidance for disciplinary actions to ensure everyone is being treated fairly.

Development of HR Policies and Procedures

The development of HR policies and procedures is a strategic process. When creating policies for the organization, the department should make sure that the policies are flexible and malleable and review them on an as-needed basis. One of the first actions that must be taken is to determine the team members who will be part of the process. Once the team has been identified and roles have been determined, that team must conduct a needs assessment. When assessing the situation, this will help HR professionals and other team members determine whether a policy is being implemented due to a change in legislation, a new procedure has been introduced, or a change in the organization requires a policy to be revised or created.

Once a needs assessment has been conducted and the policy has been determined, the writing process can begin. Once the policy has been written and approved, it can be implemented.

HR Strategy-

HR strategy is a roadmap for solving an organization's biggest challenges with people-centric solutions. This approach requires HR input during policy creation and elevates the importance of recruitment, talent management, compensation, succession planning and corporate culture.

An HR strategy-

An HR strategy is an organized set of HR methods designed to support high-performance work and promote the company's vision, mission, values, and objectives. HR may create a strategy for a single job or a collection of jobs to address specific needs within each department.

HR strategies aim to drive overall business success by spurring employees to provide high-quality work. In SHRM's guide on Human Resource strategy, Patrick M. Wright outlines three crucial elements successful HR strategies focus on:

- Have something. What skills, competencies, and abilities can employees offer?

- Feel something. What level of commitment, engagement, and motivation do your people demonstrate?
- Do something. How do your people demonstrate productivity?

Importance of HR strategy-

An HR strategy guides HR professionals toward reaching business objectives while aligning with company values. The strategy enables efficient use of the budget and effective management of HR processes. Implementing an HR strategy that focuses on nurturing community, autonomy, employee-company value alignment, and employee growth can increase retention, engagement, productivity, performance, and profit.

An HR strategy plan-

An HR strategy plan paints a picture of where your organization is currently and helps identify how to reach your goals. Consider using a SWOT analysis to help evaluate your organization's goals, create new ones, and match the right people to the roles that best utilize their skill sets. HR strategy plans can also help you determine which new positions to open and what kinds of programs will support your people as your company evolves.

The benefits of strategic human resource planning-

Strategic human resource planning enables companies to visualize and capitalize upon their current strengths and anticipate future challenges.

Some benefits of strategic human resource planning are:

- Boosting the bottom line with targeted budget allocation
- Reducing staff turnover
- Increasing team engagement and productivity
- Attracting top talent

Development of an effective HR strategy-

HR leaders can develop a thorough and dynamic HR strategy by:

- **Carving out time to plan.** Dedicate several focused hours to home in on pertinent questions, research external factors, and outline the strategy. Documenting essential information and goals helps pave a smoother path for implementing the strategy.
- **Creating a checklist.** Developing an HR strategy plan can feel overwhelming—there is a lot of information to include in such a comprehensive document. Breaking the task into smaller categories by drafting a checklist enables HR professionals to develop a well-rounded strategy with all the essential components.

- **Aligning with other business leaders.** Every successful HR strategy must align with the company's overall business strategy. In today's ever-changing work world, it's best practice to build a people-first and agile business strategy built to adapt to unforeseen challenges.
- **Creating a timeline.** The timeline should identify goals that HR leaders aim to reach throughout the year and in the long term. Routinely reassessing milestones can help companies stay on track while adjusting to unpredictable changes in the market.

Best practices for implementing an HR strategy

No one can predict how and how often the market and needs of the company will change. But, staying proactive can keep you one step ahead and ready to pivot at the drop of a hat. These guidelines can help build a proactive HR strategy:

Work with other company leaders. HR strategy serves as the foundation of a people-focused business strategy and requires the collaboration of HR and other leaders from across an organization.

- **Secure your budgets.** Allocating a budget to HR programs is critical. Work with your finance team to secure a budget and ensure your programs have the financial support they need to be successful.
- **Constantly review your strategy.** To keep up with changing business needs, it's crucial to review your strategy frequently. This will enable you to identify elements that must be updated and adjust KPIs when necessary.
- **Encourage cross-team collaboration and transparency.** The best people strategies support cross-team collaboration, liquid teams, and transparency. This approach nurtures trust and team building. It also enables companies to shift gears quickly and leverage their workforce's skill set, avoiding the need for large-scale layoffs and massive recruitment efforts with every market change.

Hierarchy of Strategy-

The hierarchy of strategies describes a layout and relations of corporate strategy and sub-strategies of the organization. Individual strategies are arranged hierarchically and logically consistent at the level of vision, mission, goals, and metrics.

Three Levels of Strategy: Corporate Strategy, Business Strategy and Functional Strategy

Strategy is at the foundation of every decision that has to be made within an organization. If the strategy is poorly chosen and formulated by top management, it has a major impact on the effectiveness of employees in pretty much every department within the organization. In our previous article on 'What is Strategy?!' we have already tried to define and explain what business strategy refers to and what is NOT considered to be part of strategy. In this article, we will dissect strategy in three different components or 'Levels of Strategy'. These three levels are: Corporate-level strategy, Business-level strategy and Functional-level strategy. Together, these three levels of strategy can be illustrated in a so called 'Strategy Pyramid' (Figure 1). Corporate strategy is different from Business strategy and Functional strategy. Even though Corporate-level strategy is at the top of the pyramid, we start this article by explaining Business-level strategy first.

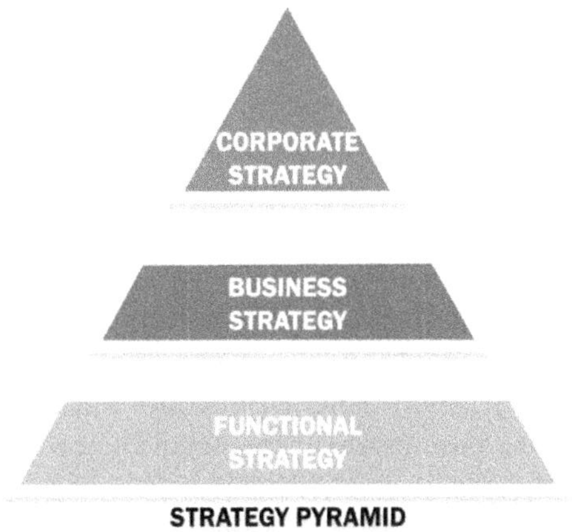

Figure 1: ***Three Levels of Strategy Pyramid***

Business-level strategy

The Business-level strategy is what most people are familiar with and is about the question "How do we compete?", "How do we gain (a sustainable) competitive advantage over rivals?". In order to answer these questions it is important to first have a good understanding of a business and its external environment. At this level, we can use internal analysis frameworks like the Value Chain Analysis and the VRIO Model and external analysis frameworks like Porter's Five Forces and PESTEL Analysis. When good strategic analysis has been done, top management can move on to strategy formulation by using frameworks as the Value Disciplines, Blue Ocean Strategy and Porter's Generic Strategies. In the end, the business-level strategy is aimed at gaining a competitive advantage by offering true value for customers while being a unique and hard-to-imitate player within the competitive landscape.

Functional-level strategy

Functional-level strategy is concerned with the question "How do we support the business-level strategy within functional departments, such as Marketing, HR, Production and R&D?". These strategies are often aimed at improving the effectiveness of a company's operations within departments. Within these department, workers often refer to their 'Marketing Strategy', 'Human Resource Strategy' or 'R&D Strategy'. The goal is to align these strategies as much as possible with the greater business strategy. If the business strategy is for example aimed at offering products to students and young adults, the marketing department should target these people as accurately as possible through their marketing campaigns by choosing the right (social) media channels. Technically, these decisions are very operational in nature and are therefore NOT part of strategy. As a consequence, it is better to call them tactics instead of strategies.

Corporate-level strategy

At the corporate level strategy however, management must not only consider how to gain a competitive advantage in each of the line of businesses the firm is operating in, but also which businesses they should be in in the first place. It is about selecting an optimal set of businesses and determining how they should be integrated into a corporate whole: a portfolio. Typically, major investment and divestment decisions are made at this level by top management. Mergers and Acquisitions (M&A) is also an important part of corporate strategy. This level of strategy is only necessary when the company operates in two or more business areas through different business units with different business-level strategies that need to be aligned to form an internally consistent corporate-level strategy. That is why corporate strategy is often not seen in small-medium enterprises (SME's), but in multinational enterprises (MNE's) or conglomerates.

Example Samsung

Let's use Samsung as an example. Samsung is a conglomerate consisting of multiple strategic business units (SBU's) with a diverse set of products. Samsung sells smartphones, cameras, TVs, microwaves, refrigerators, laundry machines, and even chemicals and insurances. Each product or strategic business unit needs a business strategy in order to compete successfully within its own industry. However, at the corporate level Samsung has to decide on more fundamental questions like: "Are we going to pursue the camera business in the first place?" or "Is it perhaps better to invest more into the smartphone business or should we focus on the television screen business instead?". The BCG Matrix or the GE McKinsey Matrix are both portfolio analysis frameworks and can be used as a tool to figure this out.

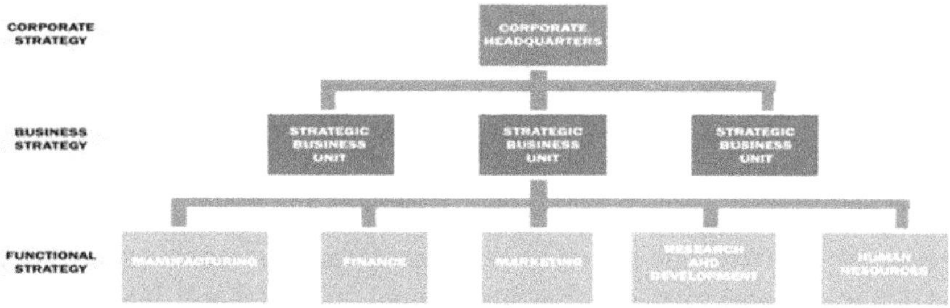

Figure 2: Hierarchy of Strategy

Role of HR in Strategic Management-

Strategic human resource management (strategic HRM) provides a framework linking people management and development practices to long-term business goals and outcomes. It focuses on longer-term resourcing issues within the context of an organisation's goals and the evolving nature of work.

Following strategic choices can be considered which would help today's organizations to survive and grow.

- **Change Management:** Manage change properly and become an effective change agent rather than being a victim of change itself.
- **Values:** Adopt proactive HRD measures, which encourage values of openness, trust, autonomy, proactivity and experimentation.
- **Maximize productivity and efficiency:** Through qualitative growth of people with capabilities and potentialities to grow and develop thrive to maximize productivity and efficiency of the organization.
- **Activities directed to competence building:** HRD activities need to be geared up and directed at improving personal competence and productive potentialities of manpower resources.

7 Key steps : Strategic Human Resource Management-

1. Develop a thorough understanding of your company's objectives
2. Evaluate your HR capability
3. Analyze your current HR capacity in light of your goals
4. Estimate your company's future HR requirements
5. Determine the tools required for employees to complete the job
6. Implement the human resource management strategy
7. Evaluation and corrective action

Even well-thought-out strategies can go askew as they evolve and change during their implementation period. Therefore, it's important that businesses have systems of evaluation and control in place to help monitor their performances. By establishing a strategic control process as a part of management, organizations can rethink strategies and take immediate actions in case of undesired or unintended outcomes.

The purpose of strategic control is to steer a business toward its long-term goal by controlling its strategic direction. Strategic control definition states that the process tracks a strategy during its implementation period and detects changes or problems that may affect the outcome. It then makes adjustments to avoid such problems. Let's discuss the meaning of strategic control, the processes involved, its importance and strategic control examples.

1. Strategic Control Meaning
2. The Strategic Control Process
3. Importance Of Strategic Control
4. Strategic Control Example

Strategic Control

Strategic control is a method of managing the execution of a strategic plan. It's considered unique in the management process, as it can handle the unknown and ambiguous while tracking a strategy's implementation and the subsequent results. In other words, strategic control is a way to find different methods of strategy implementation by adapting to changing external and internal factors to achieve strategic goals.

A strategy is usually implemented over a significant period of time during which two major questions are answered:

a. Is strategy implementation taking place as planned?
b. Taking the observed results into consideration, does the strategy require changes or adjustments?

The strategic control definition shows us that it's an evaluation exercise focused on achieving the strategic goals set by an organization. The process is crucial in bridging gaps and adapting to changes during the implementation period.

The Strategic Control Process

Every technique of strategic evaluation follows the same method. Here are the six steps involved in the strategic control process:

1. **Determining What To Control**

   Prioritize evaluation of elements that relate directly with the mission and vision of the organization and which can affect the organization's goals.

2. **Setting Standards**

   Past, present and future actions must be evaluated. Setting qualitative or quantitative control standards help in determining how managers can evaluate progress and measure goals.

3. **Measuring Performance**

   Measuring, addressing and reviewing performance on a monthly or quarterly basis can help determine a strategy's progress and ensure that standards are being met.

4. **Comparing Performance**

   Performance comparison is done to determine if an organization is falling short of the set benchmark and if these gaps between target and actuals are normal for that industry.

5. **Analyzing Deviations**

   If there are deviations, managers have to analyze performance standards and determine why performance was below par.

6. **Corrective Action**

   If a deviation is due to internal factors such as resource shortage, then managers can act to sort them out. But if it's caused by external factors that are beyond one's control, then incorrect actions can worsen the outcome.

Traditional control concepts have to be replaced by the strategic control process, as it recognizes the unique needs of long-term strategies.

Importance of Strategic Control

Let's look at the importance of strategic control:

- **Measuring Progress**

  Strategic control can help measure organizational progress. As a strategy is chosen or implemented, an outcome is determined based on the likeliness. In strategic management, it's important to measure results during and after implementation. This allows timely corrective actions as well.

- **Feedback For Future Actions**

  Since strategic management is continuous, it helps in recycling actions that are essential for achieving the objectives of an organization. This acts as inputs for making adjustments and implementing them in other future processes.

- **Rewards And Recognition Based On Performance**

  A reward system based on performance that recognizes employees throughout the implementation period is crucial for performance, desired outcome and talent retention.

The purpose of strategic control is to let managers identify changes in circumstances and allow them to modify strategies.

Operational Control System-

Operational control involves control over intermediate-term operations and processes but not business strategies. Operational control systems ensure that activities are consistent with established plans. Mid-level management uses operational controls for intermediate-term decisions, typically over one to two years.

Levels and Types of Control

Strategic Control

Managers want to know if the company is headed in the right direction and if current company trends and changes are keeping them on that right path. To answer this question requires the implementation of strategic control. Strategic control involves monitoring a strategy as it is being implemented, evaluating deviations, and making necessary adjustments.

Strategic control may involve the reassessment of a strategy due to an immediate, unforeseen event. For example, if a company's main product is becoming obsolete, the company must immediately reassess its strategy.

Implementing a strategy often involves a series of activities that occur over a period. Managers can effectively monitor the progress of a strategy at various milestones, or intervals, during the period. During this time, managers may be provided information that helps them determine whether the overall strategy is unfolding as planned.

Strategic control also involves monitoring internal and external events. Multiple sources of information are needed to monitor events. These sources include conversations with customers, articles in trade magazines and journals, activity at trade conferences, and observations of your own or another company's operations. For example, Toyota gives tours of its plants and shares the "Toyota Way" even with competitors.

The errors associated with strategic control are usually major, such as failing to anticipate customers' reaction to a competitor's new product. BlackBerry had a strong position in the business cell phone market and did not quickly see that its business customers were switching to the iPhone. BlackBerry could not recover.

Operational Control

Operational control involves control over intermediate-term operations and processes but not business strategies. Operational control systems ensure that activities are consistent with established plans. Mid-level management uses operational controls for intermediate-term decisions, typically over one to two years. When performance does not meet standards, managers enforce corrective actions, which may include training, discipline, motivation, or termination.

Unlike strategic control, operational control focuses more on internal sources of information and affects smaller units or aspects of the organization, such as production levels or the choice of equipment. Errors in operational control might mean failing to complete projects on time. For example, if salespeople are not trained on time, sales revenue may fall.

Tactical Control

A tactic is a method that meets a specific objective of an overall plan. Tactical control emphasizes the current operations of an organization. Managers determine what the various parts of the organization must do for the organization to be successful in the near future (one year or less).

For example, a marketing strategy for a wholesale bakery might be an e-commerce solution for targeted customers, such as restaurants. Tactical control may involve regularly meeting with the marketing team to review results and would involve creating the steps needed to complete agreed-upon processes. Tactics for the bakery strategy may include the following:

- building a list of local restaurants, hotels, and grocery stores
- outlining how the bakery website can be used to receive orders
- personally visiting local executive chefs for follow-up
- monitoring the response to determine whether the sales target is met

Strategic control always comes first, followed by operations, and then tactics. For example, a strategy to be environmentally responsible could lead to an operations decision to seek Leadership in Energy and Environmental Design (LEED) certification. This is a program that awards points toward certification for initiatives in energy efficiency, such as installing timed thermostats, using occupant sensors to control lighting use, and using green cleaning products. The tactical decision is deciding which energy-efficient equipment to purchase. At each level, controls ask if the decisions serve the purpose: actual energy savings, the LEED certification, and acting responsibly for the environment.

Top-Down Controls

Top-down controls are also known as bureaucratic controls. Top-down control means the use of rules, regulations, and formal authority to guide performance. It includes things such as budgets, statistical reports, and performance appraisals to regulate behavior and results. Top-down control is the most common process, where senior executives make decisions and establish policies and procedures that implement the decisions. Lower-level managers may make recommendations for their departments, but they follow the lead of senior managers.

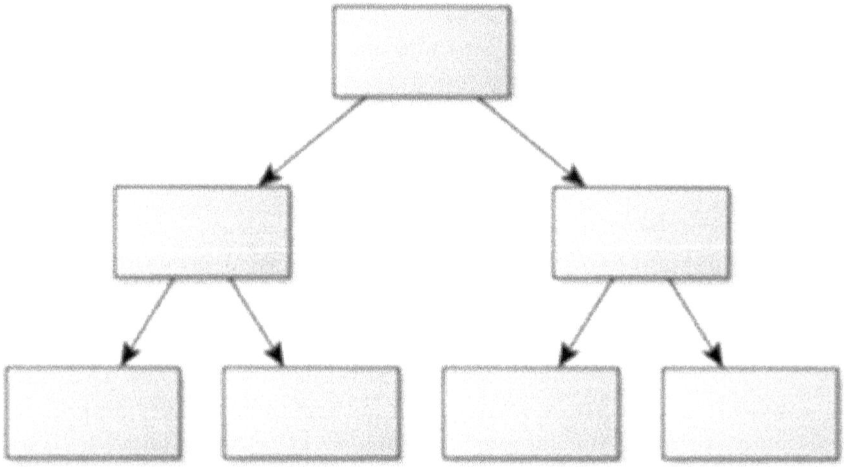

Advantages: With top-down control, employees can spend their time performing their job duties instead of discussing the direction of the company and offering input into the development of new policies. Senior executives save time by not explaining why some ideas are used and not others. Heavily regulated businesses may find this approach to be most beneficial.

Disadvantages: The top-down approach has its drawbacks. The lower levels of a company are in touch with customers and recognize new trends or new competition earlier than senior management. A heavy-handed top-down approach may discourage employees from sharing information or ideas up the chain of command.

Objective and Normative Control

Objective control is based on facts that can be measured and tested. Rather than create a rule that may be ambiguous, objective controls measure observable behavior or output. As an example of a behavioral control, let's say that a store wants employees to be friendly to customers. It could make that a rule as stated, but it may not be clear what that means and is not measurable. To make that goal into an objective control, it might specify, "Smile and greet anyone within 10 feet. Answer customer questions."

Output control is another form of objective control. Some companies, such as Yahoo, have relaxed rules about work hours and focus on output. Because programmers' output can be measured, this has worked well, whether an employee works the traditional 9 a.m. to 5 p.m. or starts at noon and works until 8 p.m.

Normative controls govern behavior through accepted patterns of action rather than written policies and procedures. Normative control uses values and beliefs called norms, which are established standards. For example, within a team, informal rules make team members aware of their responsibilities. The ways in which team members interact are developed over time. Team members come to an informal agreement as to how responsibilities will be divided, often based on the perceived strengths of each team member. These unwritten rules are normative controls and can powerfully influence behavior.

Unit III

HUMAN RESOURCE PROCUREMENT

Human resource procurement is the process of acquiring the services of employees. It includes the identification of the need for employees, solicitation and negotiation of qualified candidates, selection and placement of employees, monitoring and evaluation of employee performance, and termination of employment.

Human resource procurement enables organizations to identify and assess the skills and abilities required to meet their workforce needs. It also helps organizations find qualified candidates who are compatible with their organizational culture and goals.

Human resource procurement is important for several reasons:

1) **Human resources are a key component of an organization's overall operation.** Hiring the right people can boost productivity and efficiency, while understaffing can lead to decreased morale, disruptions in operations, and increased costs.
2) **Human resources are responsible for implementing policy directives and carrying out assigned tasks.** In order for policies to be effective, they must be implemented by skilled personnel who adhere to company standards. If there is a shortage of qualified personnel, it can make it difficult or impossible to carry out necessary tasks.
3) **Human resources help organizations develop new products and services.** Without a sufficient pool of talented individuals from which to draw on, innovation may be hindered or even prevented altogether. In addition, good human resources management can help attract top talent to an organization, thereby boosting its competitiveness in the marketplace.

Benefits of HRP

Human resource procurement is the process of identifying, recruiting and selecting the best people to fill positions in an organization. It involves making sure that the right candidates are found and hired, and that they are compatible with the company's culture and goals. HRP also includes ensuring that employees are treated fairly and with respect.

The benefits of HRP include:

1. **Increased efficiency.** HRP helps companies find the best candidates faster, which saves time and money. In addition, a well-managed HRP system can help reduce turnover rates, which saves businesses money on training costs, recruitment expenses and other associated costs.
2. **Improved morale and productivity.** When employees feel respected and appreciated, they're more likely to be productive in their jobs. A well-managed HRP system can also help create a positive work environment which leads to increased employee satisfaction and loyalty. This ultimately leads to increased productivity and lower employee turnover rates.
3. **Reduced risk of lawsuits or grievances filed by employees.** If an employee feels mistreated or harassed in their workplace, they're more likely to file a lawsuit or grievance against their employer. A well-managed HRP system can help avoid such incidents by ensuring that all candidates are interviewed objectively and that any complaints or concerns about potential hires are investigated promptly.

Types of Human Resources

Human resources procurement is the process of identifying, locating, and hiring employees. It can be broken down into two main categories: active and passive. Active human resource procurement is when a company actively goes out and looks for new employees. Passive human resource procurement is when a company uses an online database or interview system to identify qualified candidates.

There are many different reasons why companies need to procure workers. Some reasons include increasing production, retaining talented employees, filling positions that have become vacant, and meeting regulatory requirements. Regardless of the reason, there are several steps that companies must take in order to successfully procure workers.

The first step is to assess the needs of the company. This can be done by conducting market research or by talking to current employees. After understanding the company's specific needs, next comes the task of identifying potential candidates. This can be done using online databases or through personal interviews with individuals who may be a good fit for the position. Once the candidates have been identified, it is important to screen them carefully and consider all aspects of their qualifications before making a decision.

Once a decision has been made on who will fill the position, it's important to keep track of them throughout their employment cycle. This includes properly budgeting for training and development programs as well as insurance coverage. It's also important to create a clear job description and communicate it clearly to potential candidates so they know what they are looking for in a job candidate. Finally,

How to Conduct a HR Process

Human resource procurement is the process of selecting, screening, and hiring employees. It includes all steps from initial job search to employee termination. HR professionals play an important role in this process by reviewing applications, conducting interviews, and making decisions about who to hire.

To conduct a successful HR process, you need to have a plan. Start by developing a list of goals for your department. These goals may include increasing productivity or reducing turnover rates. Next, create a timeline for completing these goals. Finally, set priorities according to how important they are to your department's overall objectives.

When you're ready to start your HR process, begin by identifying your recruitment sources. This includes both internal and external candidates. Once you've identified your candidates, start the screening process by reviewing their resumes and interviewing them in person or over the phone. Finally, make a decision about who to hire and notify them of your decision.

Conclusion

HR procurement is one of the most important functions within a company. It is responsible for managing and acquiring the workforce that will help to drive success in business. By understanding what HR procurement is, why it's important, and how to go about completing an effective HR procurement process, you can ensure that your company enjoys optimal performance.

Productivity-

The Bureau of labor Statistics defines productivity as "a measure of economic performance that compares the amount of goods and services produced (output) with the amount of inputs used to produce those goods and services."

When people think of "being productive," they often think about what they're personally getting done. For many people, that means checking things off the "to-do" list. That type of personal productivity reflects how efficient you are at completing tasks. But not all tasks are created equal.

Different perspectives on productivity

Politicians, economists, and pundits talk about it at a macro level. Business leaders and managers worry about it in terms of their teams and employees working in a hybrid environment. And most of us, individually, make some assessment as to whether we "felt" very productive on a given day.

Each of these examples incorporates a different view of productivity. Here are a few examples of different perspectives on productivity.

Personal productivity

Productivity can mean different things in different contexts, especially with the rise of knowledge work and automation. Personal productivity refers to how consistently and efficiently an individual completes tasks or accomplishes goals.

Understanding the different layers of productivity can help you see how your personal productivity at work contributes to your business's productivity and maybe even how both relate to your country's productivity.

National productivity

For countries, productivity measures how well they turn labor and materials (the input) into goods and services (the output, gross domestic product [GDP]). It's a broad measure that reflects trends in policy and technology and indicates economic growth relative to other things happening in the macro-environment. This can ladder to a higher standard of living for the residents of that country.

Business productivity

For businesses, too, productivity measures how well they generate revenue from input, labor, and materials. Business productivity usually refers to productivity as revenue divided by hours worked. For company leaders, an aggregate productivity level isn't likely to provide actionable insights, but it can help them see how they compare against the competition or other leading firms.

Organizational productivity

Productivity at the company level – revenue relative to employee labor hours in a quarter – can seem far removed from our own activities, which might see results or deliver value in a different timeframe.

What is productivity in the workplace?

Workplace productivity is the value each team brings to the success of the overall business. It measures the output of individuals or teams to better understand how an organization can optimize its workflow.

Importance of productivity-

Fostering employee productivity that drives business outcomes is an essential part of business success. And it also has a positive impact on employees.

- **For businesses:** Productivity growth signifies the health and growth of the company. A productive business can expand, offering new services and potentially lowering prices.

- **For employees:** Productivity is important because it keeps individuals progressing toward their full potential. Being productive allows us to manage our work, home lives, hobbies, and family commitments with ease and peace of mind.

How to measure productivity

Unfortunately, personal productivity, at work or in life, can be hard to pin down, especially now that many people don't do repetitive tasks — it was much easier when productivity could be measured by how many widgets a person built per hour.

Personal productivity is a topic of some disagreement in the age of knowledge work. Creativity and innovation, even excellent customer service, don't neatly sum up to an efficiency metric. Nonetheless, it's useful to think about what productivity means in your role and type of work. Then try to set the conditions to improve it — whatever the metric:

- What is the appropriate way to assess quality or value?
- What is the relevant measure of quantity?
- What are the inputs we want to use most efficiently?

For your teams and for yourself, the most relevant output to think about is value. Productivity = (value of work) / (employee time, effort).

Value might seem hard to define, but you can start by thinking about outcomes. Something is valuable to you (or to a company) when it helps you achieve your desired outcomes. Not everything on your task list is equivalent in terms of the value it delivers to you or others.

This changes the way we think about productivity to incorporate how effectively an activity delivers value in addition to how efficiently we do that activity. In a company, the value of work is a function of how well the work aligns with the organization's priorities, the quality it is executed at, and the efficiency with which it is done.

The benefits of improved productivity

Being more productive is a common goal, but it's also a goal that many people struggle with.

Only 21% of UK office workers report that they are productive all day, and the average actual productive time in an 8-hour workday is 2 hours and 53 minutes.

Naturally, the challenges employees face with productivity ultimately reflect in the company's overall output, too.

- **Increased efficiency:** By being more personally productive, people can complete their work efficiently, tackle errands quicker, and enjoy more free time.

- **Improved employee well-being:** Productivity can help employees enforce healthy work/life boundaries and feel more in control of their circumstances. Some people may even enjoy their work more when they're productive, and they're likely to feel less stressed, too.
- **Improved individual and company performance:** Traditionally, we associate productivity with performance. Each person's productivity and performance contribute to business success, leading to lower prices, higher profitability, and potentially higher pay for employees.
- **Enhanced scalability:** When a business has high productivity levels, it uses its resources more efficiently and is poised for growth and expansion.

Factors affect employee productivity-

A lot goes into creating a work environment that fosters productivity. Here are some of the most common factors we've seen companies enhance to engage and motivate their employees to embrace a productive work culture.

Work environment

An employee's work environment has a huge impact on their well-being and performance. It includes many elements, such as management styles, company values, company culture, communication styles, leadership, and trust in the workplace. Investing in improving each of these areas helps avoid a toxic work environment and boosts productivity.

Growth opportunities

Many individuals are motivated by career growth and professional development opportunities. They like to be challenged, work on interesting projects, feel like their work is valued, and be rewarded for their impact. To build momentum among teams and increase productivity, try building out your career growth paths.

Opportunities to socialize

Not everyone wants to work in an office every day. And there are individuals who would rather not participate in group events. But creating opportunities for employees to meet, either in person or virtually, is important. Socialization helps build trust, increase creativity, boost collaboration, and bolster communication across teams. These events can be social or work-related team-building activities.

Manager and peer feedback

Employees thrive in organizations with healthy feedback cultures. In fact, a recent survey showed that 72% of employees consider recognition the most impactful element of employee engagement. This is not to say that all feedback has to be praise. But ensuring that there are regular check-ins with employees and offering opportunities for them to give feedback can help increase productivity.

Psychological safety

Psychological safety directly correlates to productivity in the workplace. Higher belonging is also positively correlated with increased focus, strategic planning, and goal attainment. These benefits make a strong case for developing a psychologically safe workplace by leveraging communication, vulnerability, and empathy.

Access to tools and systems

Another important factor in developing a more productive team is improving their digital employee experience. This involves offering the tools individuals need to do their work most efficiently. They can be transactional such as sales enablement tools, or focused on maximizing soft skills such as project management and collaboration tools.

Additionally, many teams function more effectively within some form of structure. So having systems and processes in place for employees to do their best work is essential.

Clear expectations

Setting and clearly communicating expectations before starting a project can save teams an immense amount of time. Investing this time upfront often cuts down on the time needed for revisions or even redos of certain tasks.

Improvement-

If you want to improve something, you've got to make improvements. Lots of people strive for personal improvement: maybe it's losing a few pounds for an improvement in their appearance, or reading more for an improvement in intelligence. Businesses look for improvement in customer service or profitability. Any change for the better or step in the right direction is an improvement.

Job Analysis-

Job analysis is the process of gathering and analyzing information about the content and the human requirements of jobs, as well as, the context in which jobs are performed.

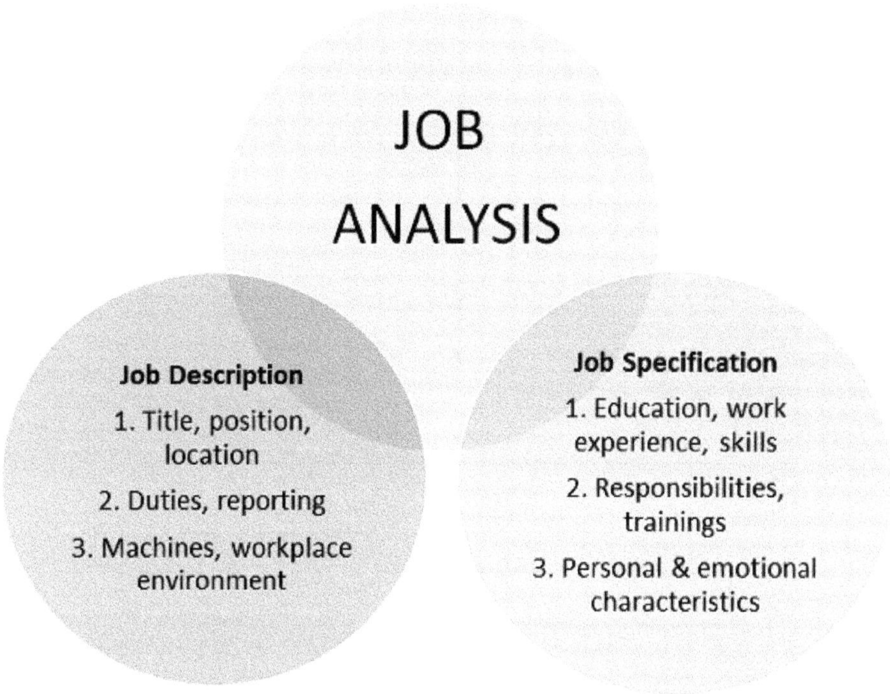

Job Analysis Process

Where to place the employees in order to best utilize their skills and talent? How to determine the need of new employees in the organization? How to eliminate unneeded jobs? How to set realistic performance measurement standards? How to identify the jobs and prepare a plan to fill them?

Well, all this can be effectively done by a proper and thorough job analysis. Managers deal such kinds of challenges in day-to-day company operations where they need to fulfill effectively and efficiently fulfill the organization's requirements related to human resource recruitment, selection, performance, satisfaction and cutting down and adding extra responsibilities and duties. And there is no scope where they can avert the risk of being wrong.

An effective and right process of analyzing a particular job is a great relief for them. It helps them maintain the right quality of employees, measure their performance on realistic standards, assess their training and development needs and increase their productivity. Let's discuss the job analysis process and find out how it serves the purpose.

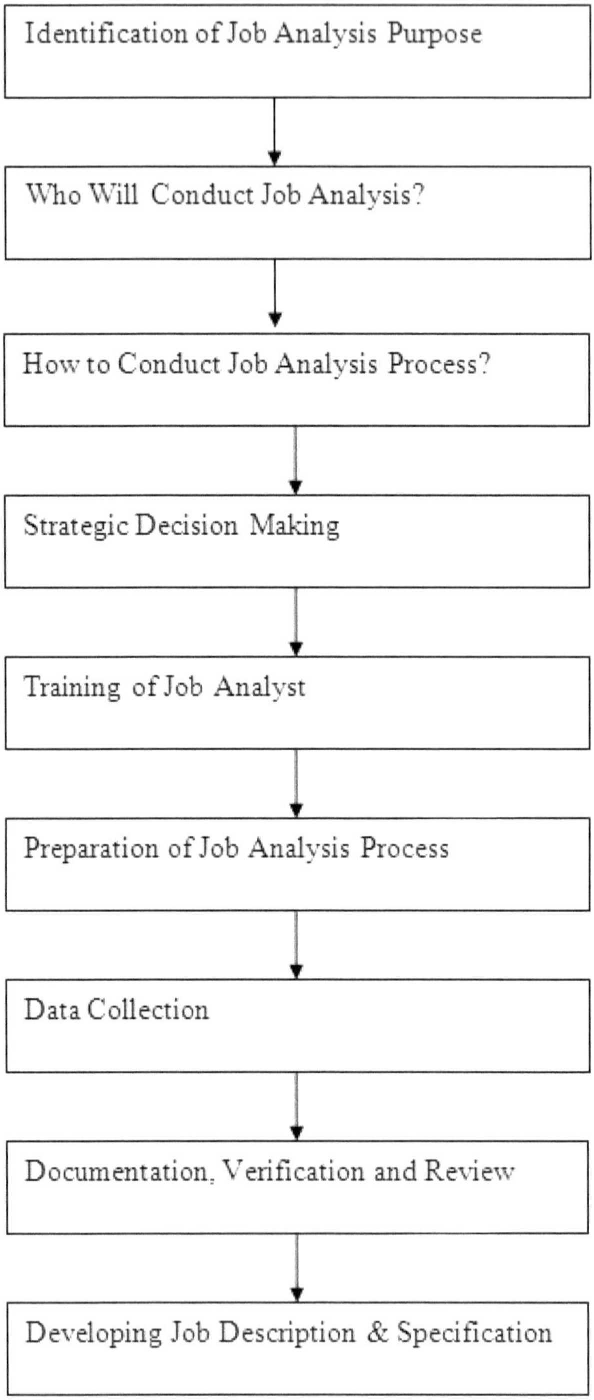
Identification of Job Analysis Purpose
Who Will Conduct Job Analysis?
How to Conduct Job Analysis Process?
Strategic Decision Making
Training of Job Analyst
Preparation of Job Analysis Process
Data Collection
Documentation, Verification and Review
Developing Job Description & Specification

- **Identification of Job Analysis Purpose:** Well any process is futile until its purpose is not identified and defined. Therefore, the first step in the process is to determine its need and desired output. Spending human efforts, energy as well as money is useless until HR managers don't know why data is to be collected and what is to be done with it.
- **Who Will Conduct Job Analysis:** The second most important step in the process of job analysis is to decide who will conduct it. Some companies prefer getting it done by their own HR department while some hire job analysis consultants. Job analysis consultants may prove to be extremely helpful as they offer unbiased advice, guidelines and methods. They don't have any personal likes and dislikes when it comes to analyze a job.
- **How to Conduct the Process:** Deciding the way in which job analysis process needs to be conducted is surely the next step. A planned approach about how to carry the whole process is required in order to investigate a specific job.
- **Strategic Decision Making:** Now is the time to make strategic decision. It's about deciding the extent of employee involvement in the process, the level of details to be collected and recorded, sources from where data is to be collected, data collection methods, the processing of information and segregation of collected data.
- **Training of Job Analyst:** Next is to train the job analyst about how to conduct the process and use the selected methods for collection and recoding of job data.
- **Preparation of Job Analysis Process:** Communicating it within the organization is the next step. HR managers need to communicate the whole thing properly so that employees offer their full support to the job analyst. The stage also involves preparation of documents, questionnaires, interviews and feedback forms.
- **Data Collection:** Next is to collect job-related data including educational qualifications of employees, skills and abilities required to perform the job, working conditions, job activities, reporting hierarchy, required human traits, job activities, duties and responsibilities involved and employee behaviour.
- **Documentation, Verification and Review:** Proper documentation is done to verify the authenticity of collected data and then review it. This is the final information that is used to describe a specific job.
- **Developing Job Description and Job Specification:** Now is the time to segregate the collected data in to useful information. Job Description describes the roles, activities, duties and responsibilities of the job while job specification is a statement of educational qualification, experience, personal traits and skills required to perform the job.

PROCESS OF JOB ANALYSIS

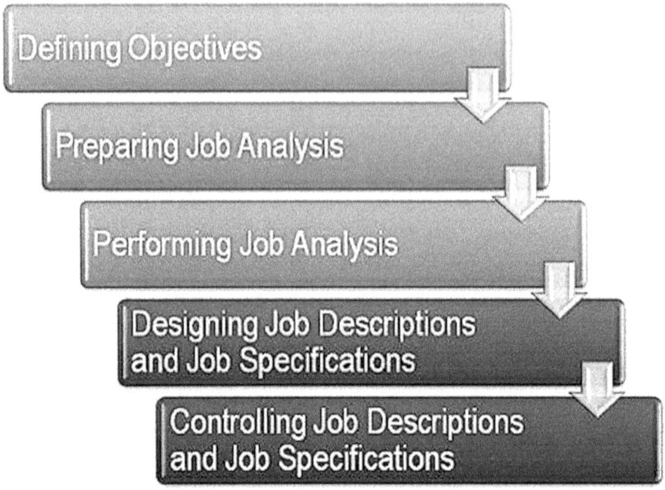

Features of Job Analysis

Job analysis is a process through which relevant information about various aspects of a job is collected and then the tasks which are to be performed are identified. It defines the role, context, conditions, behaviour, performance standards and responsibilities of a job in a systematic manner.

The objective of a job analysis is to get a deeper understanding of the job and use the information in creating job descriptions, job design, performance appraisals, worker training, workforce planning, or to make the job safer.

Purpose or Objective of Job Analysis

Factors affecting Job Design

A well defined job will make the job interesting and satisfying for the employee. The result is increased performance and productivity. If a job fails to appear compelling or interesting and leads to employee dissatisfaction, it means the job has to be redesigned based upon the feedback from the employees.

Broadly speaking the various factors that affect a job design can classified under three heads. They are:

1. Organizational Factors
2. Environmental Factors
3. Behavioural Factors

1. Organizational Factors

Organizational factors that affect job design can be work nature or characteristics, work flow, organizational practices and ergonomics.

1. **Work Nature:** There are various elements of a job and job design is required to classify various tasks into a job or a coherent set of jobs. The various tasks may be planning, executing, monitoring, controlling etc and all these are to be taken into consideration while designing a job.
2. **Ergonomics:** Ergonomics aims at designing jobs in such a way that the physical abilities and individual traits of employees are taken into consideration so as to ensure efficiency and productivity.
3. **Workflow:** Product and service type often determines the sequence of work flow. A balance is required between various product or service processes and a job design ensures this.
4. **Culture:** Organizational culture determines the way tasks are carried out at the work places. Practices are methods or standards laid out for carrying out a certain task. These practices often affect the job design especially when the practices are not aligned to the interests of the unions.

2. Environmental Factors

Environmental factors affect the job design to a considerable extent. These factors include both the internal as well as external factors. They include factors like employee skills and abilities, their availability, and their socio economic and cultural prospects.

0. **Employee availability and abilities:** Employee skills, abilities and time of availability play a crucial role while designing of the jobs. The above mentioned factors of employees who will actually perform the job are taken into consideration. Designing a job that is more demanding and above their skill set will lead to decreased productivity and employee satisfaction.

1. **Socio economic and cultural expectations:** Jobs are nowadays becoming more employee centered rather than process centered. They are therefore designed keeping the employees into consideration. In addition the literacy level among the employees is also on the rise. They now demand jobs that are to their liking and competency and which they can perform the best.

3. Behavioural Factors

Behavioural factors or human factors are those that pertain to the human need and that need to be satisfied for ensuring productivity at workplace. They include the elements like autonomy, diversity, feedback etc. A brief explanation of some is given below:

0. **Autonomy:** Employees should work in an open environment rather than one that contains fear. It promotes creativity, independence and leads to increased efficiency.
1. **Feedback:** Feedback should be an integral part of work. Each employee should receive proper feedback about his work performance.
2. **Diversity:** Repetitive jobs often make work monotonous which leads to boredom. A job should carry sufficient diversity and variety so that it remains as interesting with every passing day. Job variety/diversity should be given due importance while designing a job.
3. **Use of Skills and abilities:** Jobs should be employee rather than process centered. Though due emphasis needs to be given to the latter but jobs should be designed in a manner such that an employee is able to make full use of his abilities and perform the job effectively.

Techniques of job design

1. Job enlargement
2. Job rotation
3. Job enrichment
4. Job characteristic theory
5. Work simplification
6. Business process re-engineering
7. Task analysis
8. Job sharing
9. Work

Job enlargement

Job enlargement means increasing the scope of a job through extending the range of its job duties and responsibilities generally within the same level and periphery. Job enlargement involves combining various activities at the same level in the organization and adding them to the existing job.

Job rotation

Job rotation is a technique used by some employers to rotate their employees' assigned jobs throughout their employment. Employers practice this technique for a number of reasons

Job enrichment

Job enrichment is a method of motivating employees where a job is designed to have interesting and challenging tasks which can require more skill and can increase pay

Job characteristic theory

Job characteristics theory is a theory of work design. It provides "a set of implementing principles for enriching jobs in organizational settings".

Work simplification

Under this method, the job is simplified by breaking it down into small sub-parts. Then, each part of the job is assigned to a worker .

Business process re-engineering

Business process re-engineering is a business management strategy originally pioneered in the early 1990s, focusing on the analysis and design of workflows and business processes within an organization.

Task analysis

Task analysis is a fundamental tool of human factors engineering. It entails analyzing how a task is accomplished, including a detailed description of both manual and mental activities, task and element.

Job sharing

Job sharing or work sharing is an employment arrangement where two people, or sometimes more, are retained on a part-time or reduced-time basis to perform a job normally fulfilled by one person working full-time. This leads to a net reduction in per-employee income.

Work

In physics, work is the energy transferred to or from an object via the application of force along a displacement. In its simplest form, for a constant force aligned with the direction of motion, the work equals the product of the force strength and the distance traveled.

Ergonomics-

Ergonomics is the process of designing or arranging workplaces, products and systems so that they fit the people who use them.

Most people have heard of ergonomics and think it is something to do with seating or with the design of car controls and instruments – and it is... but it is so much more. Ergonomics applies to the design of anything that involves people – workspaces, sports and leisure, health and safety.

Ergonomics (or 'human factors' as it is referred to in North America) is a branch of science that aims to learn about human abilities and limitations, and then apply this learning to improve people's interaction with products, systems and environments.

Ergonomics aims to improve workspaces and environments to minimise risk of injury or harm. So as technologies change, so too does the need to ensure that the tools we access for work, rest and play are designed for our body's requirements.

Objective of Ergonomics-

Ergonomics is designing a job to fit the worker so the work is safer and more efficient. Implementing ergonomic solutions can make employees more comfortable and increase productivity.

The objectives of the study of ergonomics is to optimize the integration of man and machine so as to improve the work rate and accuracy.

It involves the design of:

(1) A work place be fitting the requirements of the work force.

Advertisements:

(2) Machinery, Equipment and control devices in such a manner in order to minimize physical and mental strain on the individuals/workers there by improving the efficiency.

(3) A conducive "environment for the execution of the task most effectively.

Though both Ergonomics and work study are complimentary and try to fit man to his machine or to fit the job to the workers, however, ergonomics in addition takes care of factors governing physical and mental strain.

Importance of Ergonomics:

Ergonomics plays a vital role in improving productivity. Though, it is fact that ergonomics itself does not produce anything. However, if properly exploited as on indispensable tool/ function in industry, it is capable of producing significant results. Importance of ergonomics as scientific discipline is improving with mechanization as indispensable strategy for survival. It is of great use for production/Industrial engineers and work study experts.

The approach in this methodology is that the problem form the point that the equipment and work places should be designed around capabilities of workmen; so that less human fatigue, error and conflict shall occur, which ultimately helps in providing job satisfaction.

Thus it is that dimension of work study technique where the aim is fitting the work to man and hence motivating man to work. Therefore ergonomics occupies same importance as designing of the product itself in the field of industrial productivity. It may be concluded that research in product development and design, management plus human factors engineering/ ergonomics should go in hard for improving the productivity in industry.

(i) **Performance factors:**

Biodynamic, biostatics, environmental factors, information handling.

(ii) **Personal characteristics:**

Work capacity, attitude skill, intelligence and anthropometry.

(iii) Attitude factors:

Job organization. It is clear from the factors mentioned above that the consideration of people in industry, in the structure set out does not conform to the structure of medical knowledge meaning there by that it is neither field of psychologist or sociologist only but some of the knowledge from all relevant fields will be required.

The discipline which embraces this area and provides acknowledging support form other areas such as human sciences is ergonomics. This is relatively a new science and is concerned with a scientific study of relationship between man and his working environment.

Work measurement

Work measurement is the application of techniques which is designed to establish the time for an average worker to carry out a specified manufacturing task at a defined level of performance.[1] It is concerned with the duration of time it takes to complete a work task assigned to a specific job. It means the time taken to complete one unit of work or operation it also that the work should completely complete in a complete basis under certain circumstances which take into account of accountants time

Usage

Work measurement helps to uncover non-standardization that exist in the workplace and non-value adding activities and waste. A work has to be measured for the following reasons:

1. To discover and eliminate lost or ineffective time.
2. To establish standard times for performance measurement.
3. To measure performance against realistic expectations.
4. To set operating goals and objectives.

Techniques

- Analytical estimating
- Predetermined motion time systems
- Standard data system
- Synthesis from elemental data
- Time study
- Work sampling

Purpose

Work Measurement is a technique for establishing a Standard Time, which is the required time to perform a given task, based on time measurements of the work content of the prescribed method, with due consideration for fatigue and for personal and unavoidable delays. Method study is the principal technique for reducing the work involved, primarily by eliminating unnecessary movement on the part of material or operatives and by substituting good methods for poor ones. Work measurement is concerned with investigating, reducing and subsequently eliminating ineffective time, that is time during which no effective work is being performed, whatever the cause. Work measurement, as the name suggests, provides management with a means of measuring the time taken in the performance of an operation or series of operations in such a way that ineffective time is shown up and can be separated from effective time. In this way its existence, nature and extent become known where previously they were concealed within the total.

Uses

Revealing existing causes of ineffective time through study, important though it is, is perhaps less important in the long term than the setting of sound time standards, since these will continue to apply as long as the work to which they refer continues to be done. They will also show up any ineffective time or additional work which may occur once they have been established.

In the process of setting standards it may be necessary to use work measurement:

To compare the efficiency of alternative methods. Other conditions being equal, the method which takes the least time will be the best method. To balance the work of members of teams, in association with multiple activity charts, so that, as nearly as possible, each member has a task taking an equal time to perform. To determine, in association with man and machine multiple activity charts, the number of machines an operative can run.

The time standards, once set, may then be used:

To provide information on which the planning and scheduling of production can be based, including the plant and labour requirements for carrying out the programme of work and the utilisation of available capacity. To provide information on which estimates for tenders, selling prices and delivery promises can be based. To set standards of machine utilisation and labour performance which can be used for any of the above purposes and as a basis for incentive schemes. To provide information for labour-cost control and to enable standard costs to be fixed and maintained. It is thus clear that work measurement provides the basic information necessary for all the activities of organising and controlling the work of an enterprise in which the time element plays a part. Its uses in connection with these activities will be more clearly seen when we have shown how the standard time is obtained.

Techniques of work measurement

The following are the principal techniques by which work measurement is carried out:

1. Time study
2. Activity sampling
3. Predetermined motion time systems
4. Synthesis from standard data
5. Estimating
6. Analytical estimating
7. Comparative estimating

Of these techniques we shall concern ourselves primarily with time study, since it is the basic technique of work measurement. Some of the other techniques either derive from it or are variants of it.

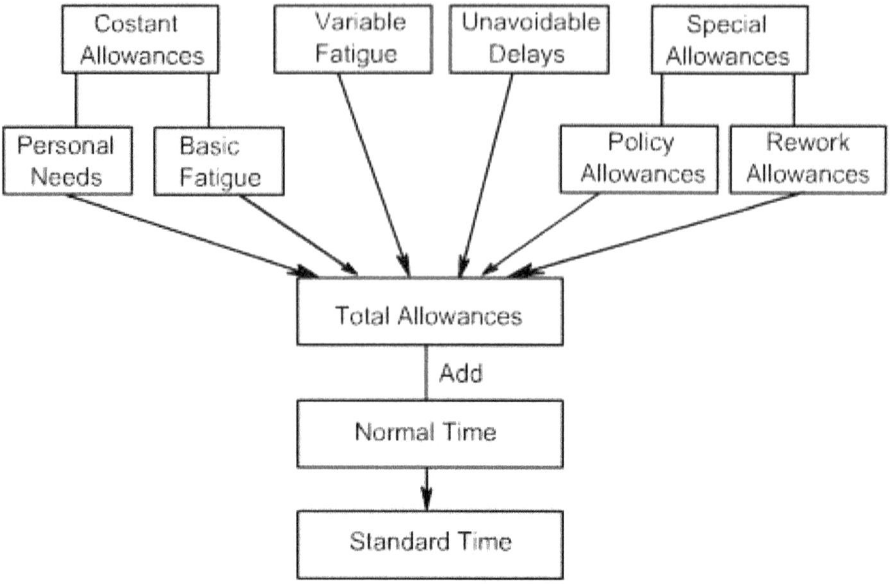

What Is Human Resource Planning (HRP)?

Human resource planning (HRP) is the continuous process of systematic planning to achieve optimum use of an organization's most valuable asset—quality employees. Human resources planning ensures the best fit between employees and jobs while avoiding manpower shortages or surpluses.

There are four key steps to the HRP process. They include analyzing present labor supply, forecasting labor demand, balancing projected labor demand with supply, and supporting organizational goals. HRP is an important investment for any business as it allows companies to remain both productive and profitable.

Key Takeaways

- Human resource planning (HRP) is a strategy used by a company to maintain a steady stream of skilled employees while avoiding employee shortages or surpluses.
- Having a good HRP strategy in place can mean productivity and profitability for a company.
- There are four general steps in the HRP process: identifying the current supply of employees, determining the future of the workforce, balancing between labor supply and demand, and developing plans that support the company's goals.

Human Resource Planning (HRP)

Human resource planning allows companies to plan ahead so they can maintain a steady supply of skilled employees. The process is used to help companies evaluate their needs and to plan ahead to meet those needs.

Human resource planning needs to be flexible enough to meet short-term staffing challenges while adapting to changing conditions in the business environment over the longer term. HRP starts by assessing and auditing the current capacity of human resources.

Here, identifying a company's skill set and targeting the skills a company needs enables it to strategically reach business goals and be equipped for future challenges. To remain competitive, businesses may need advanced skills or to upskill their employees as the market environment evolves and changes.

To retain employees and remain competitive, HRP often looks at organizational design, employee motivation, succession planning, and increasing return on investment overall.

Challenges of Human Resource Planning (HRP)

The challenges to HRP include forces that are always changing. These include employees getting sick, getting promoted, going on vacation, or leaving for another job. HRP ensures there is the best fit between workers and jobs, avoiding shortages and surpluses in the employee pool.

To help prevent future roadblocks and satisfy their objectives, HR managers have to make plans to do the following:

- Find and attract skilled employees.
- Select, train, and reward the best candidates.
- Cope with absences and deal with conflicts.
- Promote employees or let some of them go.

Investing in HRP is one of the most important decisions a company can make. After all, a company is only as good as its employees, and a high level of employee engagement can be essential for a company's success. If a company has the best employees and the best practices in place, it can mean the difference between sluggishness and productivity, helping to lead a company to profitability.

Four Steps to Human Resource Planning (HRP)

There are four general, broad steps involved in the human resource planning process. Each step needs to be taken in sequence in order to arrive at the end goal, which is to develop a strategy that enables the company to successfully find and retain enough qualified employees to meet the company's needs.

Analyzing labor supply

The first step of human resource planning is to identify the company's current human resources supply. In this step, the HR department studies the strength of the organization based on the number of employees, their skills, qualifications, positions, benefits, and performance levels.

Forecasting labor demand

The second step requires the company to outline the future of its workforce. Here, the HR department can consider certain issues like promotions, retirements, layoffs, and transfers—anything that factors into the future needs of a company. The HR department can also look at external conditions impacting labor demand, such as new technology that might increase or decrease the need for workers.

Balancing labor demand with supply

The third step in the HRP process is forecasting the employment demand. HR creates a gap analysis that lays out specific needs to narrow the supply of the company's labor versus future demand. This analysis will often generate a series of questions, such as:

- Should employees learn new skills?
- Does the company need more managers?
- Do all employees play to their strengths in their current roles?

Developing and implementing a plan

The answers to questions from the gap analysis help HR determine how to proceed, which is the final phase of the HRP process. HR must now take practical steps to integrate its plan with the rest of the company. The department needs a budget, the ability to implement the plan, and a collaborative effort with all departments to execute that plan.

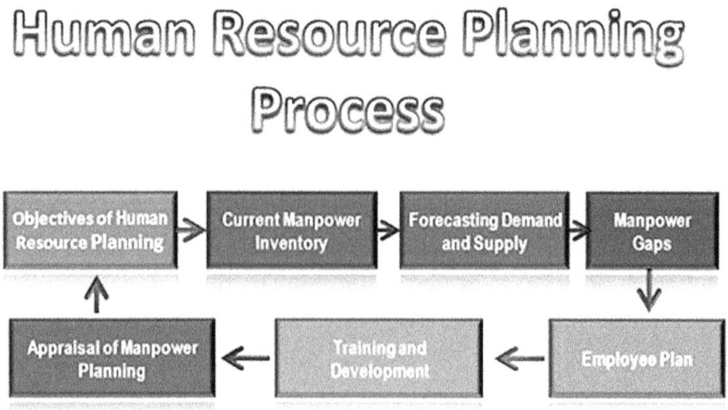

12 features of human resource management are;

1. Human Resource Management Is An Art and A Science.
2. Human Resource Management Is Pervasive
3. HRM Is A Service Function
4. HRM is a Process
5. HRM Is A Continuous Process
6. HRM Must Be Regulation-Friendly.
7. HRM is An Interdisciplinary and Fast-Changing
8. Human Resource Management is Focused On Results.
9. Human Resource Management is People-Centered
10. Human Relations Philosophy
11. HRM Is An Integrated Concept
12. HRM Develops Team Spirit

Objectives of Human Resource Planning

Everything you need to know about the objectives of human resource planning. Human resource planning comprises putting the right number and kind of people at the right place, at the right time, and making them do things for which they are suited, to achieve business goals.

In the era of industrialization, structured HR planning has become a really important aspect. It is carried out in a particular sequence of steps which begins with analysing the current inventory of manpower available.

The managers need to suitably make plans for future requirements, by forecasting along with developing employment and training programmes.

According to Coleman, "Human resource planning is the process of determining manpower requirements and the means for meeting those requirements in order to carry out the integrated plan of the organisation."

Objectives:

1. **Provide Information:**

   The information obtained through HRP is highly important for identifying surplus and unutilised human resources. It also renders a comprehensive skill inventory, which facilitates decision making, like, in promotions. In this way HRP provides information which can be used for other management functions.

2. **Effective Utilisation of Human Resource:**

   Planning for human resources is the main responsibility of management to ensure effective utilisation of present and future manpower. Manpower planning is complementary to organisation planning.

3. **Economic Development:**

At the national level, manpower planning is required for economic development. It is particularly helpful in the creating employment in educational reforms and in geographical mobility of talent.

4. **Determine Manpower Gap:**

Manpower planning examine the gaps in existing manpower so that suitable training programmes may be developed for building specific skills, required in future.

5. **To Forecast Human Resource Requirements:**

HRP to determine the future human resource needed in an organisation. In the absence of such a plan, it would be difficult to have the services of the right kind of people at the right time.

6. **Analyse Current Workforce:**

HRP volunteers to assist in analysing the competency of present workforce. It determines the current workforce strengths and abilities.

7. **Effective Management of Change:**

Proper HR planning aims at coping with severed changes in market conditions, technology products and government regulations in an effective way. These changes call for continuous allocation or reallocation of skills evidently in the absence of planning there might be under utilization of human resource.

8. **Realizing Organizational Goals:**

HRP helps the organization in its effectively meeting the needs of expansion, diversification and other growth strategies.

Human Resource Planning

Types of Planning

- Aggregate planning
  - Anticipates needs for groups of employees in specific, usually lower level jobs and general skills employee need to ensure sustained high performance
- Succession planning
  - Focuses on key individuals management positions that the organization needs to make sure remain filled and the type of individuals who might provide the best fit in these critical positions.

7 Factors Affecting HRP

These are some factors affecting HRP:

1. Type and Strategy of the Organization
2. Organizational Growth Cycles and Planning
3. Environmental Uncertainties
4. Time Horizons
5. Type and Quality of Information
6. Nature of Jobs Being Filled
7. Outsourcing

Requisites for Successful HRP (Human Resource Planning)

1. HRP must be recognized as an integral part of corporate planning
2. Support of top management is essential
3. There should be some centralization with respect to HRP responsibilities in order to have co-ordination between different levels of management.
4. Organization records must be complete, up to date and readily available.
5. Techniques used for HR planning should be those best suited to the data available and degree of accuracy required.
6. Data collection, analysis, techniques of planning and the plan themselves need to be constantly revised and improved in the light of experience.

Barriers or Limitations of Human Resource Planning

- Uncertainties: ...
- Inaccurate Forecasting Methods: ...
- Lack of Support from Top Management: ...
- Inadequate Information System: ...
- Employee Resistance: ...
- Employers' Resistance: ...
- Time-Consuming and High Cost: ...
- Lack of Participation and Coordination among Operating Managers:

Recruitment

Recruitment refers to the process of identifying, attracting, interviewing, selecting, hiring and onboarding employees. In other words, it involves everything from the identification of a staffing need to filling it.

Depending on the size of an organization, recruitment is the responsibility of a range of workers. Larger organizations may have entire teams of recruiters, while others only a single recruiter. In small outfits, the hiring manager may be responsible for recruiting. In addition, many organizations outsource recruiting to outside firms. Companies almost always recruit candidates for new positions via advertisements, job boards, social media sites, and others. Many companies utilize recruiting software to more effectively and efficiently source top candidates. Regardless, recruitment typically works in conjunction with, or as a part of Human Resources.

According to Edwin B. Flippo, "It is a process of searching for prospective employees and stimulating and encouraging them to apply for jobs in an organisation." He further elaborates it, terming it both negative and positive.

Recruitment Process

The major steps of the recruitment process are stated as:

1. Job Design
2. Opening Job Position
3. Collecting and Presenting Job Resumes
4. Job Interviews
5. Job Offer

Job Design

Job design is the most important part of the recruitment process. The job design is a phase about the design of the job profile and a clear agreement between the line manager and the HRM Function.

The Job Design is about the agreement about the profile of the ideal job candidate and the agreement about the skills and competencies, which are essential. The information gathered can be used during other steps of the recruitment process to speed it up.

Techniques of job design

1. Job enlargement
2. Job rotation
3. Job enrichment
4. Job characteristic theory
5. Work simplification
6. Business process re-engineering
7. Task analysis
8. Job sharing
9. Work

Job Enrichment

Job enrichment is a strategy used to motivate employees by giving them increased responsibility and variety in their jobs. The idea is to allow employees to have more control over their work. By doing so, one can tap into their natural desire to do a good job and contribute to the overall goals of the company.

Job Enlargement

Job Enlargement is the horizontal expansion of a job. It involves the addition of tasks at the same level of skill and responsibility. It is done to keep workers from getting bored. It is different than job enrichment.

Examples: Small companies may not have as many opportunities for promotions, so they try to motivate employees through job enlargement. Beside that if there is shortage or suffering from dearth of staff, in such case additional duties and responsibilities would be added to available employees which amount to job enlargement.

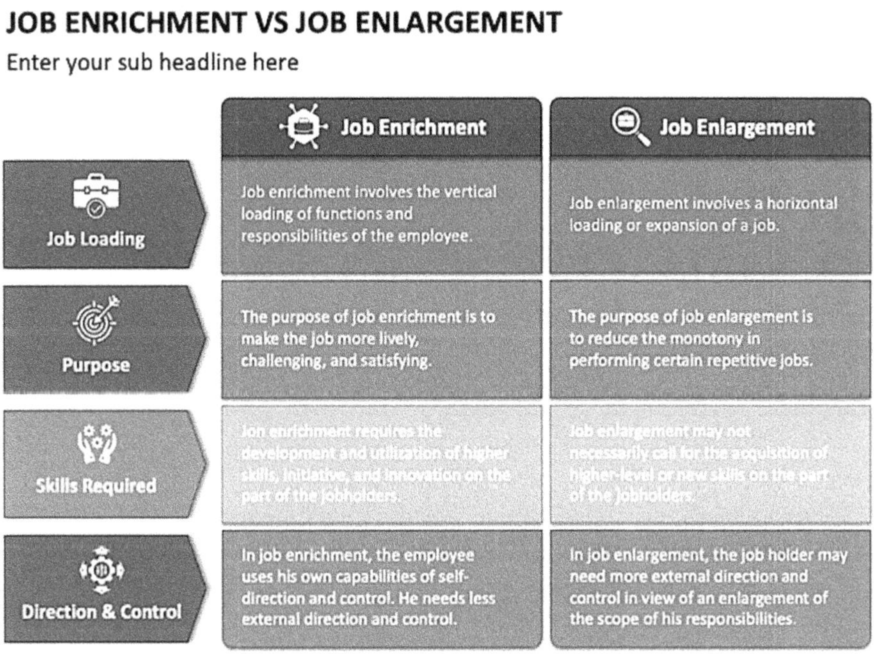

Opening Job Position

The Opening of the Job Position is generally the job of the HR Recruiter. Skilled and experienced HR Recruiter should decide about the right mix of recruitment sources to find the best candidates for the job position. This is another key step in the recruitment process.

Collecting and Presenting Job Resumes

The next step is collecting of job resumes and their pre-selection. This step in the recruitment process is very important today as many organizations lose a lot of time in this step.

Today, the organization cannot wait with the pre-selection of the job resumes. Generally, this should be the last step done purely by the HRM Function.

Job Interviews

The job interviews are the main step in the recruitment process, which should be clearly designed and agreed between HRM and line management.

The job interview should discover the job candidate, who meets the requirements and fits best the corporate culture and the department.

Job Offer

The job offer is the last step of the recruitment process, which is done by the HRM Function, it finalizes all the other steps and the winner of the job interviews gets the offer from the organization to join.

Recruitment Techniques

Recruitment techniques are the means or media by which management contacts prospective employees or provide necessary information or exchange ideas or stimulate them to apply for jobs.

Recruitment techniques are:

1. **Internal Methods:** They are for recruiting internal candidates. These include methods like:

   (a) Promotion & Transfers

   (b) Job Posting

   (c) Employee Referrals

2. **Direct Methods:** These include sending travelling recruiters to educational and professional institutions and employees' contacts with the public.

   (a) Campus Recruitment

Nature of Recruitment

Recruitment involves the following features:

- Recruitment is the first step of appointment.
- It is a continuous process.
- It is a process of identifying sources of human force, attracting and motivating them to apply for jobs in organizations.

- It is a development manpower or to work at the last stage.
- It is a positive process.
- It fulfills needs, both the present, and the future.

Purpose of Recruitment

- Finding out and developing the source here required number and kind of employees will be available.
- Developing suitable techniques to attract the desirable candidate.
- Employing the technique to attract employees.
- Stimulating as many candidates as possible and asking them to apply for jobs irrespective of the number of candidates required in order to increase the selection ratio (i.e., number of application per one job vacancy) due to lower yield ratio.

Difference Between Recruitment and Selection

- Recruitment means searching for sources of labor and stimulating people to apply for jobs, whereas selection means selecting of right kind of people for various jobs.
- Recruitment is a positive process whereas selection is a negative process.
- It creates a large pool of applicants whereas selection leads to a screening of unsuitable candidates.
- Recruitment is a simple process, it involves contracting the various sources of labor whereas selection is a complex and time-consuming process. The candidate has to clear a number of hurdles before they are selected for a job.

Sources of Recruitment

A source from where candidates are identified, attracted and selected can be classified into two: Internal Sources and External Sources.

Modes of Recruitment are:

1. Transfers
2. Promotions
3. Retired and Retrenched Employees
4. Employee Referrals
5. Job Postings
6. Deceased and Disabled Employees
7. Campus Recruitments
8. Management Consultants

9. Advertisements
10. Trade Associations
11. Walk in Interview
12. Job Fairs

Internal Sources

This approach includes recruiting, developing and promoting the employees from within the organization. Internal recruitments are cost-effective, more reliable as the organization is aware of the candidate's skillset and knowledge and it also motivates the employees and increases their commitment towards the organization. Internal sourcing can be done in the following ways:

Transfers

An employee may be shifted from one job to another internally generally of the same level. The roles and responsibilities of the employees might change but not necessarily the salary. This helps the employees to get motivated and try something new, helps them break the monotony of the old job and encourages them to grow by gaining more knowledge.

Promotions

As recognition of their efficiency and experience the employees are moved from a position to a higher position. There is a change in their duties and responsibilities accompanied with a change in salary and status. It helps the employee to grow vertically in the organization. It refrains him from leaving the company for greener pastures.

Retired and Retrenched Employees

Retired and retrenched employees may also be recruited back in case there is high demand and shortage of supply in the industry or there is sudden increase in work load. These employees are already aware of the processes, procedures and culture of the organization hence they prove to be cost effective.

Employee Referrals

In this case each employee of the company acts as a recruiter. The employees are encouraged to recommend the names of their friends or relatives working in other organizations. For this they are even rewarded monetarily.

The benefit of employee referral is that the potential candidate gets first hand information about the job and organization culture from the already working employee. Since he knows what he is getting into he is expected to stay longer in the organization. Also since the credibility of those who recommend is at stake, they tend to recommend those who are highly motivated and competent.

Job Postings

The Company posts the current and expected vacancy on bulletin boards, electronic media and similar common portals. This gives an opportunity to the employees to undertake career shift and help them grow within the company.

Deceased and Disabled Employees

In order to make the families of the deceased and disabled employees self-sufficient their relatives or dependents may be offered a job in case of any vacancy.

Advantage of Internal Sourcing

- Internal recruitment is less time consuming and economical.
- It is reliable as the organization is aware of the employee's knowledge and skill set.
- There is no need of induction and training as the employee is already aware of the processes, procedures and culture of the organization.
- It increases the motivation level of the employees as they look forward to getting a higher job in the organization instead of looking for greener pastures outside.
- It boosts the morale of the employees, improves their relations with the organization and reduces employee turnover.
- It develops the spirit of loyalty in the employees, ensures continuity of employment and organizational stability.

Disadvantage of Internal Sourcing

- Internal sourcing prevents new blood, originality and innovative ideas from entering the organization.
- The scope is limited as not all the vacancies can be filled by the limited pool of talent available in the organization.
- The position of the person who is transferred or promoted falls vacant.
- It can create dissatisfaction amongst the rest of the employees as there can be bias or partiality in promoting an employee in the organization.

External Sources

New candidates are recruited from outside the organization by different means and methods. It is more commonly used than internal sources. External recruitments are helpful in acquiring skills that are not possessed by the current employees; it also helps to bring onboard employees from different backgrounds that get a diversity of ideas on the table.

Campus Recruitments

When companies are in search of fresh talents and are focusing on knowledge, communication skill and talent than experience, they approach management colleges, technical institutes etc. The company makes a presentation about its organization in order to attract the students.

Whoever finds it matching with their career plans applies for the job. These applicants are then made to go through series of selection processes like analytical and psychological tests, group discussions, interviews etc before the final selection is done.

Management Consultants

Management consultants act as representatives of the employer. They perform the recruitment function on behalf of the client company by charging them fees or commissions. These consultants are able to tailor their services according to the specific needs of the clients thus relieving the line managers from their recruitment function.

Advertisements

This media of recruitment is very popular and commonly used as it reaches out a wide range of people. It can also be targeted at a specific group or a particular geographic area by choosing a specific newspaper, radio channel etc. e.g Business journal.

In certain advertisements company name, job description and salary packages are mentioned. There are blind advertisements as well where no identification of the firm is given. These advertisements are published mostly when the organization wants to fill an internal vacancy or planning to displace an existing employee.

Trade Associations

There are associations that create a database of job seekers and provide it to its members during regional or national conventions. They also publish classified advertisements for employers interested in recruiting their members.

Walk in Interview

Another upcoming method of recruitment is walk-in interviews. There is no time and meeting schedule for each individual. An advertisement regarding the time and the location of the interview is given in the newspaper. The candidates are required to carry their CVs and directly appear for the interview. It is a very common mode of recruitment amongst BPOs and call centres.

Job Fairs

Job fairs are an effective way of getting in touch with potential employees and candidates. There are HR hiring managers of various companies under one roof. Information and business cards can be exchanged and resumes can be submitted by the candidates.

Employers can spot the right applicants, similarly the applicants can apply in many organizations together, wherever they feel the offer is best and suits their interest.

Advantage of External Sourcing

- New and young blood enters the organization, which have innovative ideas, new approaches that can help to stir up the existing employees.
- It offers a wider pool for selection. Companies can pick up candidates with requisite qualification.
- It creates a competitive environment as it helps the existing employees to work harder in order to match the standard that the new employees bring in.
- It leads to long term benefits to the organization. Talented pools of people bring along with them new methods of working and new approaches to situations that helps the organization to stay abreast with the competitive world outside.

Disadvantage of External Sourcing

- It is a time consuming process as it involves attracting the right candidates, screening them, going through a series of tests and interviews etc. When suitable candidates are not available this process has to be repeated again and again.
- This process proves to be very expensive for the organization as the companies have to resort to advertisements, hiring consultants etc for attracting the right pool of talent.
- It can lower the morale and demotivate the existing employees as they can feel that their services have not been recognized.
- It is less reliable than internal sourcing. Since the organizations hire candidates on the basis of their resumes, tests, interviews etc they may not turn out to be as expected. It may end up hiring someone who ends up being a misfit and may not be able to adjust in the new set up.

Alternatives to Recruitment

Recruitment and selection is a costly and time-consuming process. Moreover, it gets onboard permanent employees which are hard to be separated in case they do not perform as per the requirement or if there is overstaffing due to less work due to market demand fluctuations.

Hence to fight back the temporary phases of high market demand for firm's products, companies might resort to alternatives to recruitment that are stated below:

1. Overtime
2. Temporary Employees
3. Sub-contracting
4. Employee Leasing
5. Outsourcing

Overtime

In order to fulfill the extra demand of the firm's products which lead to excess work load, some employees are asked to work overtime under some terms and conditions. Overtime is the amount of time that someone works beyond the working hours.

In such a case employee gets extra wages as per the contract signed between the employee and the employer. The disadvantage is that the employee might not work to his full potential during the day in order to earn overtime.

Temporary Employees

A temporary employee is appointed for a period that does not last for long. It is to fill a short term position which is scheduled to be terminated within one or more years for reasons as the completion of a specific project or peak workload.

This helps the company in avoiding expenses of recruitment, saves time involved, and help avoid the negative impact of labor turnover etc. However temporary employees might not be very loyal to the company, their inexperience may affect the work output and they tend to take time to adjust.

Sub-contracting

To complete a specific project or fulfill a sudden temporary increase in the demand of the company's products, the company might resort to subcontracting. It is the practice of assigning part of the obligations, tasks and responsibilities to another party under a contract known as subcontractor.

Hiring an outside specialist agency to undertake part of the work leads to mutual advantages in such cases as the company would like to expand on its own only when the increased demand lasts for a specified period of time.

Employee Leasing

An employee leasing firm specializes in recruitment, training, human resource management, payroll accounting and risk administration. The leasing firm also takes care of the work supervision, daily duties and other routine aspects of work.

For example a nursing services firm hires many nurses and provides them to hospitals on a contract basis. It provides an advantage to the organization to change its employees without actual layoffs.

Outsourcing

Under outsourcing a business process is contracted out to a third party, the reason behind outsourcing are many. It reduces the need to hire and train specialized staff as it is sourced out to someone specializing in that area possessing the resources and expertise that leads to competitive superiority over time.

It also helps to reduce capital and operating expenses and helps avoid burdensome regulations, high taxes, labour union contracts etc.

Role Profiles for Recruitment Purposes

Role profiles, define the overall purpose of the role, its reporting relationships and key result areas. They may also include the list of competencies required. They may be technical (skills and knowledge required to do a specific job) and behavioral competencies attached to the role.

The profile also includes the terms and conditions (pay, benefits, hours of work, mobility, travelling, transfers, training, development and career opportunities). The recruitment role provides the basis for person specification.

Person Specifications

A person specification also known as recruitment, job or personnel specification is the essential element on which the selection procedure is based. It is the sum total of education, training, experience, qualification a person has to perform the job assigned to him.

When the job requirement have been specified, they should be categories under suitable heads. The basic categories include qualification, technical and behavioural competencies.

There are also a number of traditional schemes. The most popular include the seven-point plan developed by Alec Rodgers in 1952 and the five-point grading system developed by Munro Fraser in 1954. These give certain headings under which attributes of an ideal candidate can be classified.

Seven Point Plan

- **Physical make up:** Health, physique, appearance, bearing and speech
- **Attainments:** Education, qualifications, experience
- **General intelligence:** Fundamental intellectual capacity
- **Special aptitudes:** Mechanical, manual dexterity, facility in use of words or figures
- **Interest:** Social, intellectual, physically active, constructional
- **Disposition:** Acceptability, influence over others, steadiness, dependability, selfreliance
- **Circumstances:** Domestic circumstances, occupations of family.

Five-fold Grading System

- **Impact on others:** Physical make-up, appearance, speech and manner
- **Acquired knowledge or qualification:** Education, vocational training, work experience
- **Innate abilities:** Natural quickness of comprehension and aptitude for learning
- **Motivation:** The kind of goals set by the individual, his or her consistency and determination in following them up, and success in achieving them
- **Adjustment:** Emotional stability, ability to stand up stress and ability to get on with people.

Attracting Candidates

Attracting candidates is primarily a matter of identifying, evaluating and using the most appropriate sources of applicants. However, where suitable sources of recruitment are not there, then the analysis of factors contributing to the recruitment in an organization need to be analyzed. Various factors to be taken under consideration are as follows:

Internal Factors

- Company's pay package
- Quality of Work Life
- Organizational culture
- Career planning & growth
- Company's size
- Company's products/services
- Company's growth rate
- Role of trade union
- Cost of recruitment
- Company's name & fame

External Factors

1. Socio-economic factors
2. Supply and demand factors
3. Employment rate
4. Labour market condition
5. Political, Legal & Govt. factors
6. Information System

Effective Recruiting

Recruitment must be speedy, but a cautious process. A wrong move can have a disastrous impact on the undertaking. A few measures can be taken to reduce the negative impact. They are:

1. Brand Image Creation
2. Stating clear Definition of Employee Requirements
3. Applications Receiving Sources
4. Screening of Applications
5. Selection Process
6. Maintain a Candidate Pool
7. Recruitment Policy
8. Internal and External Sources

Human Resource Planning

1. What is Human Resource Planning?
2. Human Resource Planning Process
3. Human Resource Demand Forecasting
4. What is Human Resource Development?
5. Challenges of Human Resource Development
6. Methods of Performance Appraisal

1. What is Job Analysis?
2. What is Job Design?
3. Recruitment Meaning
4. Effective Recruiting
5. Selection Process
6. What is Employee Induction?

Human Resource Management

Selection Process

The selection process can be defined as the process of selection and shortlisting of the right candidates with the necessary qualifications and skill set to fill the vacancies in an organisation. The selection process varies from industry to industry, company to company and even amongst departments of the same company.

Every organisation creates a selection process because they have their own requirements. Although, the main steps remain the same. So, let's understand in brief how the selection process works.

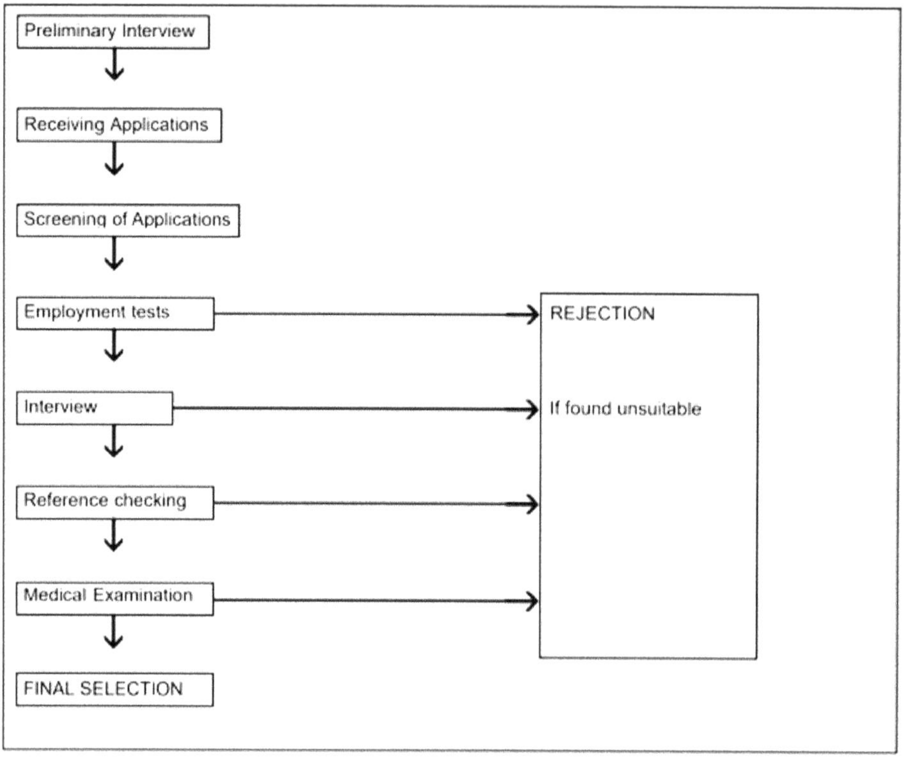

Objective-

The purpose of selection process is to pick up the most suitable candidate who would meet the requirements of the job in an organization best, to find out which job applicant will be successful, if hired.

Purpose of selection process

The purpose of selection process is to pick up the most suitable candidate who would meet the requirements of the job in an organisation best, to find out which job applicant will be successful, if hired. To meet this goal, the company obtains and assesses information about the applicants in terms of age, qualifications, skills, experience, etc. the needs of the job are matched with the profile of candidates. The most suitable person is then picked up after eliminating the unsuitable applicants through successive stages of selection process. How well an employee is matched to a job is very important because it is directly affects the amount and quality of employee's work and overall performance and productivity of the organization.

Any mismatch in this regard can cost an organisation a great deal of money, time and trouble, especially, in terms of training and operating costs. In course of time, the employee may find the job distasteful and leave in frustration. He may even circulate 'hot news' and juicy bits of negative information about the company, causing incalculable harm to the company in the long run. Effective election, therefore, demands constant monitoring of the 'fit' between people the job.

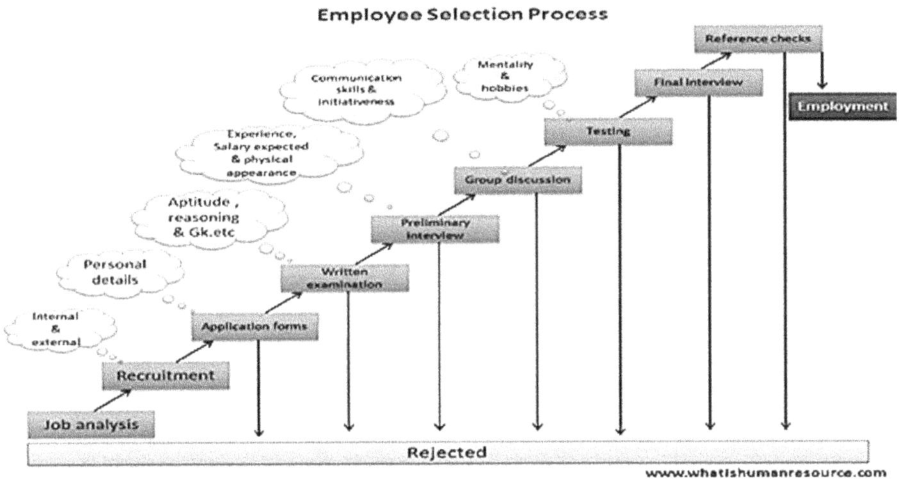

Career Planning-

The career planning process is when you figure out what you want your career path to look like and what you have to do to make it happen. You set short, medium, and long-term career goals, then determine the steps you need to take to accomplish those goals

1. A career may be defined as ' a sequence of jobs that constitute what a person does for a living'.
2. According to Schermerborn, Hunt, and Osborn, 'Career planning is a process of systematically matching career goals and individual capabilities with opportunities for their fulfillment'.

The major objectives of career planning are as follows:

- To identify positive characteristics of the employees.
- To develop awareness of each employee's uniqueness.
- To respect feelings of other employees.
- To attract talented employees to the organization.
- To train employees towards team-building skills.
- To create healthy ways of dealing with conflicts, emotions, and stress.

Career Planning

Career planning is a process of identifying the professional path that would suit your personality, interests and goals. It involves exploring different career options, performing a self-evaluation to test your suitability for these and finding the right ways to get on a career track. For instance, you can find out which educational qualifications you would need for your career, what type of training you can take and what professional opportunities might be available to you later.

6 Steps for Career Planning

- Step 1: Explore Career Options. ...
- Step 2: Conduct Field Research. ...
- Step 3: Determine Your Job Target. ...
- Step 4: Build Your Credentials and Resume. ...
- Step 5: Prepare for Your Job Search. ...
- Step 6: Launch Your Job Search.

Career Development-

According to Middlemist, Hill and Greer, "Career development is a process of planning the series of possible jobs one may hold in an organization over time and development strategies designed to provide necessary job skills as the opportunities arise".

Objectives-

The purposes and objectives of career development programme, therefore, can be listed as follows: To attract and retain effective persons in an organization. To utilize human resources optimally. To improve morale and motivation level of employees.

Various benefits of career development which are as follows:

Reduces attrition of employees:

A career development program helps to increase the level of satisfaction of the employees and therefore reduce the number of people who intend to leave the organization.

Provides equal opportunity employment:

There is the chance for equal opportunity employment when one considers the career development program since these programs identify each person for the merits. Highly effective people and the results that are shown by the individual are taken as a criterion for their development and not other criteria; which therefore demonstrate equal opportunity.

Improves the use of the employees:

Career development enables employees to learn better aspects of their work and improve their capabilities. It also helps them to manage their time efficiently and ensure that the use of employees increases over time.

Improves the quality of the work-life of employees:

Career Development helps employees learn better methods of working, work ethics and other important aspects of work.

Improves the organization itself:

Through a career development program, employees have increased knowledge of the various activities of the firm. Therefore the sharing of knowledge and work ethics tends to make the organization improve.

Increases the skill of the employees:

An employee's skill improves if he/she goes through a career development program. These programs aim at increasing various facets of a worker's life which makes the latter perform better at work.

Importance of Career Development:

Understanding the importance of career development is very necessary for both parties, it's a pdf download above links. Business Environment Factors that can Bring Undesired Changes;

Cost Reduction Strategies of the Organization:

Cost-reduction strategies of the organizations are again very dangerous for those individuals; who are not prepared to move on to the next level. If organizations have to cut down their operating costs; the employment of those individuals is at stake; who are not employable or who have not performed up to the mark in the past. Employees continuously need to upgrade themselves and show their talent to remain in the organization for a long.

Economic Downsizing:

The biggest of all the factors that have badly affected the careers of millions of individuals is economic downsizing. The jobs are cut from the organizations and the fittest of all employees survive. If employees continuously learn new and better skills, chances are that economic conditions won't hurt them that badly as compared to other individuals.

IT Innovations:

Continuous changes and up-gradation in technology are also some of the major factors that bring change. Some individuals can keep pace with the changing technology and are always ready to learn and adopt new IT applications; while some show immense resistance which is not acceptable to the organizations. Employees need to keep themselves updated and show the willingness to accept changes as and when they occur and mold themselves accordingly.

De-layering:

De-layering means reclassification of jobs. This is an organizational change initiative where a company decides to reclassify the jobs more broadly. However, old reporting lines do exist to maintain managerial control but some jobs may remove or cut down during the process. Again, those individuals have to leave the organization; who are not competent enough to be shifted to another job with a different nature.

Stages of career development

1. Establishment stage
2. Mid career
3. Late career
4. Exploration stage
5. Late career stage
6. Preparation stage
7. Retention stage
8. Commitment stage
9. Transition stage
10. Investigation stage
11. Goal
12. Career exploration

Training-

Training constitutes a basic concept in human resource development. It is concerned with developing a particular skill to a desired standard by instruction and practice. Training is a highly useful tool that can bring an employee into a position where they can do their job correctly, effectively, and conscientiously. Training is the act of increasing the knowledge and skill of an employee for doing a particular job.

Definition of Training:

Dale S. Beach defines training as 'the organized procedure by which people learn knowledge and/or skill for a definite purpose'. Training refers to the teaching and learning activities carried on for the primary purpose of helping members of an organization acquire and apply the knowledge, skills, abilities, and attitudes needed by a particular job and organization.

According to Edwin Flippo, 'training is the act of increasing the skills of an employee for doing a particular job'.

Need for Training:

Every organization should provide training to all the employees irrespective of their qualifications and skills.

Specifically the need for training arises because of following reasons:

1. **Environmental changes:**
   Mechanization, computerization, and automation have resulted in many changes that require trained staff possessing enough skills. The organization should train the employees to enrich them with the latest technology and knowledge.

2. **Organizational complexity:**
   With modern inventions, technological upgradation, and diver¬sification most of the organizations have become very complex. This has aggravated the problems of coordination. So, in order to cope up with the complexities, training has become mandatory.

3. **Human relations:**
   Every management has to maintain very good human relations, and this has made training as one of the basic conditions to deal with human problems.

4. **To match employee specifications with the job requirements and organizational needs:**
   An employee's specification may not exactly suit to the requirements of the job and the organization, irrespective of past experience and skills. There is always a gap between an employee's present specifications and the organization's requirements. For filling this gap training is required.

5. **Change in the job assignment:**

   Training is also necessary when the existing employee is pro¬moted to the higher level or transferred to another department. Training is also required to equip the old employees with new techniques and technologies.

Importance of Training:

Training of employees and mangers are absolutely essential in this changing environment. It is an important activity of HRD which helps in improving the competency of employees. Training gives a lot of benefits to the employees such as improvement in efficiency and effectiveness, development of self confidence and assists every one in self management.

The stability and progress of the organization always depends on the training imparted to the employees. Training becomes mandatory under each and every step of expansion and diversification. Only training can improve the quality and reduce the wastages to the minimum. Training and development is also very essential to adapt according to changing environment.

Types of Training:

Various types of training can be given to the employees such as induction training, refresher training, on the job training, vestibule training, and training for promotions.

Some of the commonly used training programs are listed below:

1. **Induction training:**

   Also known as orientation training given for the new recruits in order to make them familiarize with the internal environment of an organization. It helps the employees to understand the procedures, code of conduct, policies existing in that organization.

2. **Job instruction training:**

   This training provides an overview about the job and experienced trainers demonstrates the entire job. Addition training is offered to employees after evaluating their performance if necessary.

3. **Vestibule training:**

   It is the training on actual work to be done by an employee but conducted away from the work place.

4. **Refresher training:**

   This type of training is offered in order to incorporate the latest development in a particular field. This training is imparted to upgrade the skills of employees. This training can also be used for promoting an employee.

5. **Apprenticeship training:**

Apprentice is a worker who spends a prescribed period of time under a supervisor.

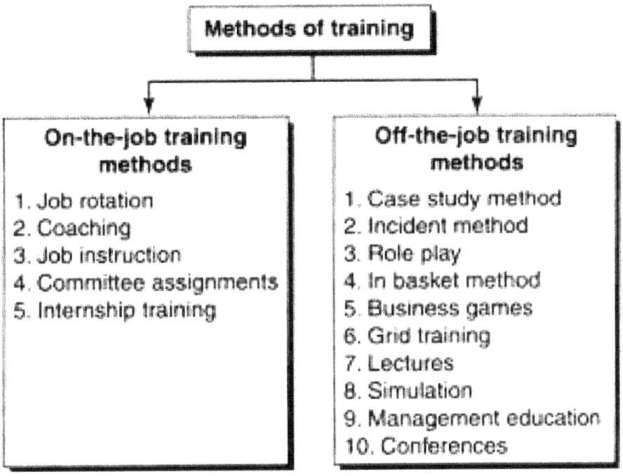

On-the-job training isn't always standard practice, but it can increase productivity and efficiency in specific industries. Not only that, it can benefit the company as a whole, from reducing training costs to creating more effective, motivated employees.

This article will cover how to begin on-the-job training for employees and how it can benefit your company and workforce. Once you read this guide, you will understand the advantages of on-the-job training and how to implement it at your workplace successfully.

Discover:

- What is on-the-job training?
- Benefits of on the job training
- On the job training plan with best practices

What is on-the-job training?

On-the-job training (OJT) is a practical approach to acquiring new competencies and skills needed for a job in a real, or close to real, working environment.

It is often used to learn how to use particular tools or equipment in a live-work practice, simulated, or training environment.

Rather than showing employees presentations or giving them worksheets, they learn about the job by doing it. This training happens at the workplace, with guidance from a supervisor, manager, or another knowledgeable employee.

New employees that undergo on-the-job training get a firsthand look at all the work procedures they can expect to encounter. They learn workplace expectations, equipment operation, and any other skill they need to complete their job successfully.

On-the-job training may take anywhere from days to weeks or longer, depending on the tasks the job requires. Often, new employees start by shadowing other employees and then move onto completing these tasks with supervision.

The importance of on the job training

There are all types of learners: some are visual, some are hands-on, and some do better by reading instructions. However, on-the-job training has incredible importance in today's workforce.

On-the-job training allows employees to gain experience working in situations very similar to those they'll encounter on a daily basis. Employees will use the same tools and equipment they need for their job while being guided by an experienced trainer.

This allows employees to learn and practice their job while still in training.

Other training methods, like online training or seminars, only give employees basic information rather than actual experience.

"Experience is the teacher of all things."

– Julius Caesar

Benefits of on the job training

On-the-job training benefits employees and employers, and this next section will highlight some of the key benefits of on-the-job training.

1. **Faster training with real experience**

   People quickly learn what they need to do and perform their job on a good or acceptable level.

   Traditional training can be a lengthy process, and employees may not retain much information. This means employees may need correction or retraining later on.

   With on-the-job training, employees learn precisely what their job entails and ask any questions that arise while shadowing coworkers.

2. **Faster adaptation to a new job**

   It is essential in industries with high turnover rates, e.g., retail, restaurant business, customer service, manufacturing, etc.

   This type of training can help with faster onboarding and getting an acceptable level of performance. It allows employees to learn processes in your organization faster and more efficiently.

3. **In most cases, it is easy to set up**

   On-the-job training is one of the simpler training programs to set up. Because you already have employees that know the job, you have a knowledge base to draw from.

   You don't need to set up complicated presentations. You simply need to pick a high-performing employee to train new staff.

4. **Trainee can perform simple job tasks from the beginning**

   Trainees start learning the easier parts of their job first. As such, they can take on small responsibilities before they even complete training.

   For instance, answering phones or directing customers to the correct store departments. If you are shorthanded and get busy, your trainee can assist, and this can ease the block in the workflow.

5. **Retain good employees**

   Employee retention is crucial in any industry. However, employees aren't as effective if they're unsure of what exactly their job entails.

   Not only that, confusion about the work expected from them can create a stressful environment, leading to high turnover rates.

   On-the-job training shows employees exactly what duties they're expected to complete, and exactly how to complete them.

   As part of their training process, they practice each task expected of them and get detailed information about what processes their job involves.

   This eliminates confusion, stress, and allows employees to perform their job to the best of their abilities.

6. **Attract the right people**

   On-the-job training allows companies to find the right people for the job because they show capability during the training process. Also, by offering on-the-job training, companies become more attractive to potential employees.

   These prospective employees know their time is well spent, and employers can assess skills during training.

7. **Team building**

   With on-the-job training, new employees meet their new coworkers right away and start becoming part of the team.

   This creates familiarity and opens up opportunities for new employees to ask questions, even if their training is complete.

   Additionally, trainees become more familiar with various workplace departments and can expand their skill set over time.

8. **Elementary knowledge management**

More experienced employees transfer their knowledge and experience to the new employees, so this knowledge wouldn't be lost if they leave the company. Of course, it doesn't cover deep or specific knowledge, but at least it is something.

Many employers refer to this as "knowledge management". Essentially, by having more experienced employees transfer their job knowledge, you retain those skills and knowledge within the company.

9. **Financial benefits**

On The Job

On-the-job training happens as part of the regular workday and requires less time. Traditional training requires set training sessions and sometimes seminars.

So the employer saves money on training, and at the same time, the employee performs some of the work duties and brings additional profit to the company.

On the job training

These tips and best practices will help you bring on-the-job training into your workplace.

1. **Identify potential trainers**

You wouldn't have a new employee perform any real job alone. So you need to find trainers who are willing to share their knowledge.

Being selected to train other employees should be an incentive for good employee performance.

Not only that, but it also shows you which experienced employees can be promoted over time.

Not all trainers must be managers. However, the employees you do select as on-the-job trainers should show exceptional performance and a high level of capability and knowledge within their job.

Some employers choose to hire third-party trainers, which can be helpful if you don't have the resources to train from within your workforce.

2. **Structure training process**

Any good training program starts with a structured plan. Create a list of the tasks the job requires on a regular basis, and detail the policies and procedures employees should know.

Because this varies with each job, you need to create a plan and list for each job.

3. **Automate the learning process**

   If you have a learning environment with training materials that can cover some aspects of the job, then provide access to it. It can save trainers time and help trainees retain needed information.

   Also, they can use it after the training to refresh knowledge, or practice something.

   Not only that, your employees will know where to turn first, before seeking other assistance and taking time from another employee's tasks.

4. **Allow trainees to practice their skills**

   After learning from their instructor, new employees should be allowed to practice their skills, under the supervision of their trainer.

   During this time, trainers should evaluate their performance. If there are any issues, the trainer can address and correct them.

   Once on-the-job training is complete, conduct an assessment to ensure the employee has gained the skills needed for their job.

5. **Check-in during and after training**

   Depending on the length of the training, it may be necessary to assess progress during the process.

   For example, evaluating the trainee's skills after learning a particular aspect of the job.

   Remember, part of the on-the-job training is ensuring that new employees have the knowledge and skills to complete their job independently.

6. **Get feedback and improve**

   After employees complete on-the-job training, get feedback from both trainer and trainee. This provides you several insights into how your on-the-job training program is working.

First, you can see how effective on-the-job training is for your company. Next, you can assess areas that may need improvement or skills that may need more time for training.

You can also get insight into how both the trainer and trainee performed. This allows you to determine whether the trainer is effective, or if another employee is better suited to the task.

Off-the-job training

Off-the-job training refers to an education method where employees learn more about their job or the latest advancements in their field at a location away from their workplace. This type of training essentially helps employees perform their job more efficiently. Unlike on-the-job training, off-the-job training can take place near the workplace or somewhere further away, such as at a resort or at a training center. When employers hold training away from the workplace, it helps minimize distractions so employees can fully focus on the material they're learning.

Off-the-job training methods

Off-the-job training is conducted in a location specifically designated for training. It may be near the workplace or away from work, at a special training center or a resort Conducting the training away from the workplace minimize distractions and allows trainees to devote their full attention to the material being taught- However, off-the-job training programs may not provide as much transfer of training to the actual job as do on-the-job programs. Many people equate off-the-job training with the lecture method, but in fact a very wide variety of methods can be used.

Definitions:

Employee training at a site away from the actual work environment. It often utilizes lectures, case studies, role playing, simulation, etc. See also on the job training.

"Off the Job Training" Methods

1. Classroom Lectures:

under the off the job methods of training, classroom method or lecture method is well-known to train white collar or managerial level employees in the organisation. under this method employees are called to the room like that of classroom to give training by trainer in the form of lectures. This method is effectively used for the purpose of teaching administrative aspects or on management subject to make aware of procedures and to give instructions on particular topic.

Advantage - It can be used for large groups. Cost per trainee is low.

Disadvantages - Low interest of employees. It is not learning by practice. It is One-way communication. No authentic feedback mechanism. Likely to lead to boredom for employees.

2. Audio-Visual:

Providing training by way of using Films, Televisions, Video, and Presentations etc. This method of training has been using successfully in education institutions to train their students in subjects to understand and assimilate easily and help them to remember forever. New companies have come up for providing audio visual material for students in their concern subjects. In the corporate sector, mainly in customer care centers employers are giving training to their employees by using audio visuals material to teach how to receive, talk and behaviour with the customer.

Training and development

Employee Training Introduction

Need and benefit of Training

Advantages Of Training Program

Training Process

- On-the-job Methods
- Off-the-job Methods

Sensitivity Training

Management Development

- On the Job Methods [MD]
- Off the Job Methods [MD]

Executive Development

Advantages - Wide range of realistic examples, quality control possible.

Disadvantages - One-way communication, No feedback mechanism. No flexibility for different audience.

3. Simulation:

The simulation Method of training is most famous and core among all of the job training methods. in the simulation training method, trainee will be trained on the especially designed equipment or machine seems to be really used in the field or job. But, those equipment or machines are specifically designed for training a trainees were making them ready to handle them in the real field or job. This method of planning is mostly used where very expensive machinery or equipment used for performing Job or to handle that job.

Example:- The simulation method has been using widely for the purpose of training aeroplane pilots on aeroplane simulator to make them ready to handle an fly aeroplane. Especially in Air force fighter pilots are getting trained on the jet fighters simulator. because the cost of aeroplane or jet fighter will be very expensive, hence employer may not allow directly to get trained on real equipment to avoid damage to equipment or machine or in sometimes may cause loss of trainee life. To avoid all such risks by the employer giving training on simulator is safe. (normally simulators for the purpose of training would be provided by the manufacturer of original equipment)

4. Vestibule Training: -

Mostly this method of training will be used to train technical staff, office staff and employees who deal with tools and machines. Employees learn their jobs on the equipment they will be using, but the training is conducted away from the actual work floor by bringing equipments or tools to certain place where training is provided, but not work place. Vestibule training allows employees to get a full feel for doing task without real world pressures. Additionally, it minimizes the problem of transferring learning to the job.

Vestibule training is provided to employees when new or advanced equipment or tools introduced in to the organisation to do a particular job by using them. For this purpose such equipment is brought to a separate place to give demonstration and train how to use and that handle it by employees safely.

5. Case Studies:

It is a written description of an actual situation in the past in same organisation or somewhere else and trainees are supposed to analyze and give their conclusions in writing. This is another excellent method to ensure full and whole hearted participation of employees and generates good interest among them. Case is later discussed by instructor with all the pros and cons of each option. It is an ideal method to promote decision-making abilities within the constraints of limited data.

6. Role Playing:

During a role play, the trainees assume roles and act out situations connected to the learning concepts. It is good for customer service and training. This method is also called 'role-reversal', 'socio-drama' or 'psycho-drama'. Here trainees act out a given role as they would in a stage play. Two or more trainees are assigned roles in a given situation, which is explained to the group. There are no written lines to be said and, naturally, no rehearsals. The role players have to quickly respond to the situation that is ever changing and to react to it as they would in the real one. It is a method of human interaction which involves realistic behaviour in an imaginary or hypothetical situation. Role playing primarily involves employee-employer relationships, hiring, firing, discussing a grievance problem, conducting a post appraisal interview, disciplining a subordinate, or a salesman making presentation to a customer.

7. Programmed Instructions:

This involves two essential elements: (a) a step-by-step series of bits of knowledge, each building upon what has gone before, and (b) a mechanism for presenting the series and checking on the trainee's knowledge. Questions are asked in proper sequence and indication given promptly whether the answers are correct.

This programme may be carried out with a book, a manual or a teaching machine. It is primarily used for teaching factual knowledge such as Mathematics, Physics, etc.

8. Management Games With computerized management games:

Trainees divide into five- or six-person groups, each of which competes with the others in a simulated marketplace. Each group typically must decide, for example.

1. how much to spend on advertising.
2. how much to produce,
3. how much inventory to maintain, and
4. how many of which product to produce.

Usually, the game itself compresses a two- or three-year period into days, weeks, or months. As in the real world, each company team usually can't see what decisions (such as to boost advertising) the other firms have made, although these decisions do affect their own sales.

Management games can be effective. People learn best by being involved, and the games can gain such involvement. They help trainees develop their problem-solving skills, as well as to focus attention on planning rather than just putting out fires. The groups also usually elect their own officers and organize themselves. This can develop leadership skills and foster cooperation and teamwork.

- Advantages of Off-the-Job Training Trainers are usually experienced enough to train
- It is systematically organized
- Efficiently created programs may add lot of value
- Disadvantages of Off-the-Job Training: It is not directly in the context of job
- It is often formal
- It may not be based on experience.
- It is expensive.
- Trainees may not be much motivated
- It is artificial in nature.

Difference Between On-the-job and Off-the-job training

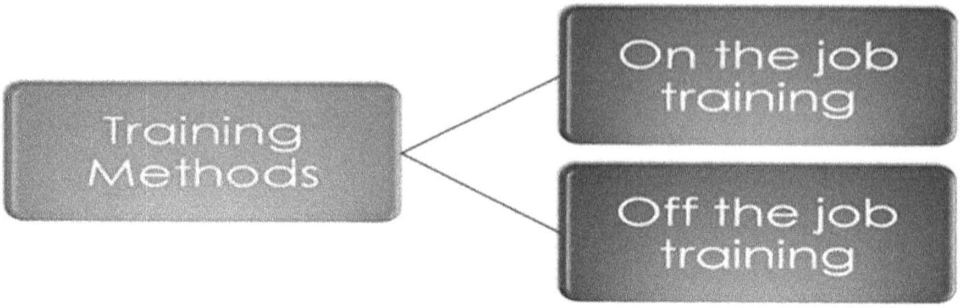

Nowadays, training has become the core needs of the organization to develop specific skills in their existing and prospective employees. There are two methods for imparting training in workers are on-the-job training and off-the-job training. As their name suggests, the former refers to the training imparted at the actual job location involving 'hands-on' training, whereas the latter method involves giving training to the employees at a place other than the real job location.

While on-the-job training is provided at the workplace itself, the trainees produce things while learning. In off-the-job training, the trainiees are away from the work environment, that eliminates stress, frustration and bustle of day-to-day job.

Dale S. Beach "*Performance appraisal is systematic evaluation of the individual with respect to his or her performance on the job and his or her potential for development*".

Comparison Chart

BASIS FOR COMPARISON	ON-THE-JOB TRAINING	OFF-THE-JOB TRAINING
Meaning	On the job training refers to a form of training which is provided at the work place during the performance of the actual job.	When the employees are given training outside the actual work location, such a type of training is termed as off the job training.
Approach	Practical	Theoretical
Active participation	Yes	No
Location	At the workplace	Away from the workplace
Principle	Learning by performing	Learning by acquiring knowledge
Work disruption	No, because trainees produce the products during learning.	Yes, because first training is provided which is followed by a performance.
Carried out by	Experienced employees	Professionals or experts.

Cost	Inexpensive	Expensive
Suitable for	Manufacturing firms	Non-manufacturing firms

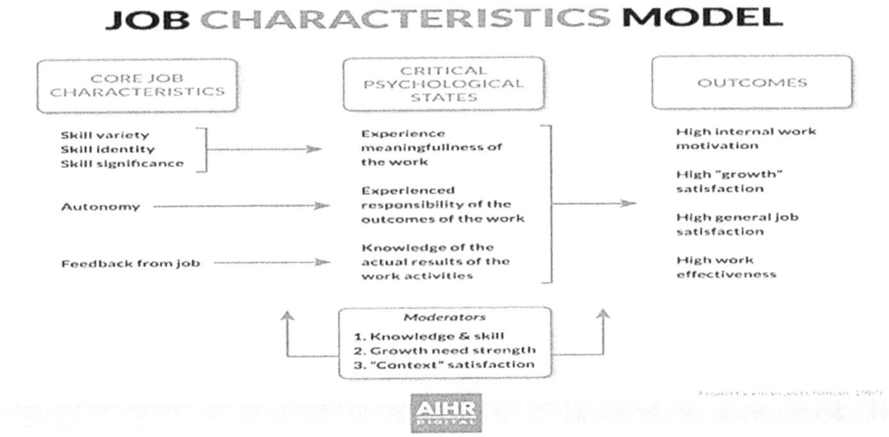

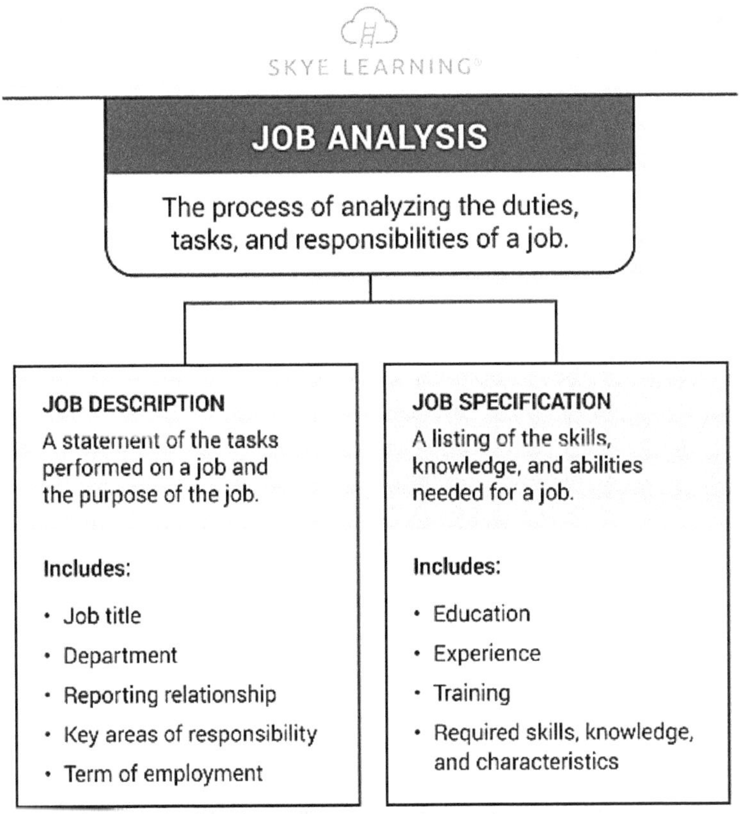

Job Description

A job description includes an overview, role summary, catalog of responsibilities, and the qualifications and experience required for a particular role. It also defines the soft skills and business skills required for success in the role. Job descriptions should be fine-tuned and reviewed with stakeholders, such as senior management, to gain consensus on the requirements of a specific position to support a company's work, behavioral and business requirements.

Job Specification

A job specification is the list of recommended qualities for a person to qualify for and succeed in a position. While the job description includes the title position, responsibilities and summary, the specification identifies the skills, traits, education and experience a candidate might need to qualify for that job. This helps outline a candidate's capabilities to perform what's listed in the job description.

Performance Appraisal-

A performance appraisal is a systematic and periodic process of measuring an individual's work performance against the established requirements of the job. It's a subjective evaluation of the employee's strengths and weaknesses, relative worth to the organization, and future development potential.

Methods of Performance Appraisals Include:

- **720-Degree feedback:** You could say that this method doubles what you would get from the 360-degree feedback! The 720-degree feedback method collects information not only from within the organization but also from the outside, from customers, investors, suppliers, and other financial-related groups.
- **The Assessment Center Method:** This method consists of exercises conducted at the company's designated assessment center, including computer simulations, discussions, role-playing, and other methods. Employees are evaluated based on communication skills, confidence, emotional intelligence, mental alertness, and administrative abilities. The rater observes the proceedings and then evaluates the employee's performance at the end.
- **Behaviorally Anchored Rating Scale (BARS):** This appraisal measures the employee's performance by comparing it with specific established behavior examples. Each example has a rating to help collect the data.
- **Checklist Method:** This simple method consists of a checklist with a series of questions that have yes/no answers for different traits.

- **Critical Incidents Method:** Critical incidents could be good or bad. In either case, the supervisor takes the employee's critical behavior into account.
- **Customer/Client Reviews:** This method fits best for employees who offer goods and services to customers. The manager asks clients and customers for feedback, especially how they perceive the employee and, by extension, the business.
- **Field Review Method:** An HR department or corporate office representative conducts the employee's performance evaluation.
- **Forced Choice Method:** This method is usually a series of prepared True/ False questions.
- **General Performance Appraisal:** This method involves continuous interaction between the manager and the employee, including setting goals and seeing how they are met.
- **Human Resource Accounting Method:** Alternately called the "accounting method" or "cost accounting method," this method looks at the monetary value the employee brings to the company. It also includes the company's cost to retain the employee.
- **Management By Objective (MBO):** This process involves the employee and manager working as a team to identify goals for the former to work on. Once the goals are established, both parties discuss the progress the employee is making to meet those goals. This process concludes with the manager evaluating whether the employee achieved the goal.
- **Performance Tests and Observations:** This method consists of an oral test that measures employees' skills and knowledge in their respective fields. Sometimes, the tester poses a challenge to the employee and has them demonstrate their skills in solving the problem.
- **Project Evaluation Review:** This method involves appraising team members at the end of every project, not the end of the business year.
- **Ratings Scales:** These ratings measure dependability, initiative, attitude, etc., ranging from Excellent to Poor or some similar scale. These results are used to calculate the employee's overall performance.
- **For organizations:** employee assessments provide insight into an employee's contribution, enabling management to improve working conditions, address behavioral issues, recognize employee talents, support skill and career development, and improve strategic decision-making.
- **For employees:** performance reviews are a way to recognize and thank them for their achievements, find opportunities for promotions or bonuses, help them get training or education to advance their careers, find

areas where they can improve, encourage and involve them in their career development, and start conversations about long-term goals.

- program requirements.
- Help make confirmation/acceptance decisions regarding employees who have completed a probationary period.
- Help make decisions regarding raising an employee's salary, offering incentives, or changing variable pay.
- Clarify expectations and facilitate communication between managers and subordinates.
- Help employees realize their whole potential performance level.
- Collect relevant employee data and keep the records for various future organizational purposes.

Traditional Methods of Employee Performance Appraisal

Here is a list of different traditional methods which can be used for employee performance appraisal:

- **Rating Scales:** In this scale, the factors such as attitude, initiative, dependability, etc are quantified. A range of excellent to poor is provided to the rater and based on the rating the performance of the employee is calculated.
- **Checklist:** A checklist form of performance appraisal consist of a column of 'Yes' and 'No' for different employee traits. The rater has to put a tick mark based on if the traits exist or do not exist in the employee.
- **Forced Choice Method:** In this method, different statements about the performance of the employee are provided to the rater and he/she is forced to answer the ready-made statements as true or false. Further evaluation of performance is carried on by the Human Resource department based on the answers of the rater.
- **Forced Distribution Method:** In this method, it is assumed that the performance of an employee conforms to a bell-shaped curve. Thus, the rater has to put employees on provided points on the scale.
- **Critical Incidents Method:** Here the critical behavior of the employee is considered by the supervisor while evaluating the performance.
- **Behaviorally Anchored Rating Scale:** Different statements which are descriptive in nature are prepared about the behavior of the employee. These behaviors are put on the scale points and the rater has to indicate the points which explain the employee behavior in a more exact way.

- **Field Review Method:** In this method, the reviewer of the performance is generally someone outside the department. The people from the HR department or corporate office do the performance evaluation of the employee based on the records and interviews.
- **Performance Tests and Observations:** This is a kind of oral test that is conducted to test the skills and knowledge of the employees in their respective fields. The employees sometimes receive a situation and are asked to demonstrate their skills and then their performance is evaluated based on that presentation.
- **Confidential Reports:** Often the government departments follow this method of performance evaluation. The employees are evaluated based on the parameters such as leadership quality, teamwork, integrity, technical ability, attendance, etc. The reviewer sends the confidential review to the concerned authority about the performance of the employee.
- **Essay Method:** Under this method, the detailed description of the employee performance is written by the rater. The performance of an employee, his relations with other Co-workers, requirements of training and development programs, strengths and weaknesses of the employee etc. are some of the points that are included in the essay. The efficiency of this traditional method of performance appraisal depends on the writing skills of the rater.
- **Cost Accounting Method:** It is a simple method in which the performance of the employee is linked with the monetary benefits of the organization. The rater checks about the cost to the company to keep the employee and the contribution of the employee in terms of monetary business.
- **Comparative Evaluation Approaches:** This approach includes a comparison of the performance of co-workers with each other. It is of two types namely the ranking method and paired comparison method. It is a quite popular method of employee performance appraisal in the corporate world.
- Modern Methods of Employee Performance Appraisal
- Here is a list of different modern methods which can be used for employee performance appraisal:
- **Management by Objectives:** In this method, the performance of the employee is assessed based on the targets achieved by him/her. The management at the beginning of the financial year conveys the set goals to the employees, at the end of the year the performance of the employee is compared with the set goals and evaluated for the appraisal.
- **Psychological Appraisals:** Psychologists are invited to the companies for the performance appraisal of the employees. Here the performance is in the context of the potential future performance. Psychological tests, in-depth

interviews, reviews, and discussions with the managers are the methods used for the evaluation of the performance.

- **Assessment Centers:** A series of exercises are conducted at the assessment center of the company to actually evaluate the performance of the employee. The exercises include discussions, role-playing, computer simulations, and many more. The employees are evaluated in terms of communication skills, mental alertness, emotional intelligence, confidence, and administrative abilities. The rater observes the event and evaluates the performance of the employee at the end.
- **360-Degree Feedback:** It is particularly a 360-degree feedback method in which the information about the performance of the employee is collected from supervisors, peers, group members, and self-assessment. All the remarks are considered to evaluate the overall work performance of the employee.
- **720-Degree Feedback:** In line with the 360-Degree feedback system, here the feedback is collected from the stakeholders within the company as well as the people linked from outside the organization. The customers, suppliers, investors, and other financial groups provide feedback about the performance of the employee.

Objectives of Employee Performance Appraisal

The main objective of the employee performance appraisal is often termed as a comparison of the standard performance set by the organization with the actual performance of the employee. However, there are some other important objectives served by the employee performance appraisal system as given below-

- The performance appraisal system maintains the records which are used to determine the compensation and wage structure of the employee.
- It is very useful to determine the strengths and weaknesses of the employees and helps to place the right person at the right job.
- It provides access to the potential in the person for future growth and development
- It gives the necessary feedback regarding the performance of the employee and their actual contribution to the growth of the organization.
- It guides the HR department about the training needs of the employees.
- It influences the working habits of the employees and makes them work-oriented.

Advantages of Performance Appraisal

- It helps the supervisors to chalk out the promotion for performing employees and dismiss the inefficient workers.
- It helps the organization to decide the compensation of the employee. Also, based on the performance and the additional efforts put by the employee the extra benefits and allowances can be decided using records of performance appraisal.
- Special actions can be taken for the development of the employees. The performance appraisal system will highlight the weakness of the employee based on which the training program arrangement can be carried out by the organization.
- The performance appraisal further suggests the changes in the selection process which will help to hire better employees.
- Performance review is an effective way to communicate the status of the performance of the employee. It is a way to provide feedback about how the employees are doing on their job.
- The evaluation of the performance can act as a motivational tool. It provides a picture of the efficiency of the employee and motivates the individual to improve their performance.

Disadvantages of Performance Appraisal

- Performance appraisal totally depends on the factors used for the evaluation of the performance. The use of incorrect or irrelevant factors can lead to the failure of performance appraisal.
- Sometimes the vital factors responsible for the performance are ignored during performance appraisal.
- The factors like attitude, abilities, and initiative are very vague and difficult to gauge.
- Sometimes the managers who carry out the performance appraisal are not qualified enough to properly assess the abilities of the employees. Thus, it leads to irrelevant data collection and failure of performance appraisal.

Promotion

Promotion is the appointment of existing members of staff to another post or office at a higher grade than the one previously held. This may be the result of either a successful application for an advertised vacancy, or, where appropriate, personal promotion.

In the words of Paul Pigors and Charles Myers, "Promotion is an advancement of an employee to a better job, better in terms of greater responsibilities, more prestige or status, greater skill and specially increased rate of pay or salary".

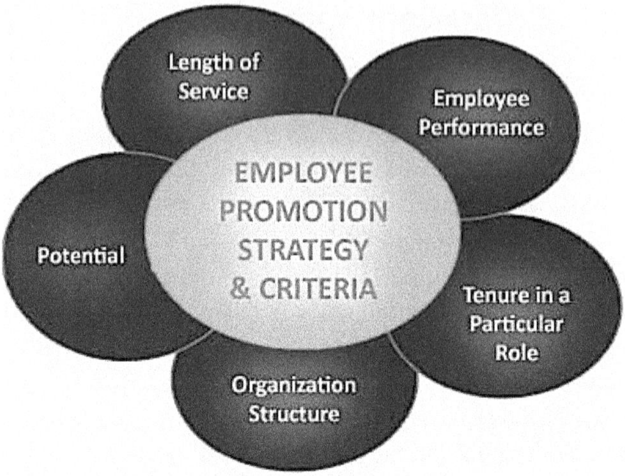

Condition of Promotion

The main conditions of promotion are given below

- Reassignment of higher level job to an employee than what he is presently performing.
- The employee will naturally be delegated with greater responsibility and authority than what he has had earlier.
- Promotion normally accompanies higher pay.

It means that in some cases, the employees perform higher level job and receive the salary related to the level of the faculty position.

Types of promotion

Promotion is mainly three types

- Vertical Promotion
- Upgraduation Promotion
- Dry Promotion

Vertical Promotion

Under this type of promotion, employee us moved to the next higher level, in the organisational hierarchy with greater responsibility, authority, pay and status.

Upgradution promotion

Under this type of promotion, the job is upgraded in the organisational hierarchy. Consequently, the employee gets more salary, higher authority and responsibility .

Dry Promotion

Under this promotion, the employee is moved to the next higher level in the organisational hierarchy with greater responsibility, authority and status without any increase in salary.

Purposes of Promotion

Organisations promote the employees with a view to achieve the following purposes:

1: To utilize the employee's skill, knowledge at the appropriate level in the organisational hierarchy resulting in organisational effectiveness and employee satisfaction.

2: To develop competitive spirit and inculcate the zeal in the employee to acquire the skill, knowledge etc., required by higher level jobs.

3: To develop competent internal source of employees ready to take up jobs at higher levels in the changing environment.

4: To promote employee's self-development and make them await their turn of promotions. It reduce labour turnover.

5: To promote a feeling of content with the existing conditions of the company and a sense of belongingness.

6: To promote interest in training, development programmes and in team development areas.

7: To build loyalty and to boost morale.

8: To reward committed and loyal employees.

9: To get rid of the problems created by the leaders of workers union by promoting them to the officers levels where they are less effective in creating problems.

Bases of Promotions

Organisation adopt different bases of promotions depending upon their nature, size, management etc. Generally, they may combine two or more basis of promotion.

Organisation should have the idea of effectiveness of each in promoting the right man to the job.

There are three bases of promotions are given below:

- Merit as a basis of promotion
- Seniority as a basis of promotion
- Seniority-cum-Merit

Base 1: Merit as a basis of promotion

Merit is taken to denote an individual employee's skill, knowledge, ability, efficiency and aptitude as measured from educational, training and past employment record.

There are many advantages of merit system of promotion are:-

1: The resources of higher order of an employee can be better utilized at higher level. It result in maximum utilization of human resources in an organisation.

2: Competent employees are motivated to expert all their resources and contribute then to the organisational efficiency and effectiveness.

3: It works as golden hand-cuffs regarding employee turnover

4: It continuously encourages the employees to acquire new skills, knowledge etc.

Base 2: Seniority as a basis of promotion

Seniority refers to relative length of service in the same job and in the same organisation. The logic behind of this base there is a positive correlation between the length of service in the same job and the amount of knowledge and the level of skill acquired by an organisation.

The advantages of seniority as a basis of promotion are:

- It is relatively easy to measure the length of service and judge the seniority.
- There would be full support of the trade unions to this system.
- Every party trust the management's action as there is no scope for favoritism and discrimination and Judgement.
- It gives a sense of certainty of getting promotion to every employee and of their turn of promotion.
- Senior employees will have a sense of satisfaction to this system as the older employees are respected and their inefficiency cannot be pointed out.
- It minimises the scope for grievances and conflicts regarding promotions.
- This system seems to serve the purpose in the sense that employees may learn more with increase in the length of service.

Base 3: Seniority-Cum-Merit

Managements mostly prefer merit as the basis of promotions as they are interested in enriching its human resources. But trade unions favor seniority as the sole basis for promotion with a view to satisfy the interests of majority of their members.

A combination of both seniority and merit can be considered as the basis for promotion satisfying the management for organisational effectiveness and the employees and trade unions for respecting the length of service.

Benefits of promotion

Promotions of employees from lower ranks to higher positions benefits the organisation as well as employees.

1: Promotion places the employees in a position where an employee's skill and knowledge can be better utilized.

2: it creates and increases the interest of other employees in the company as they believe that they will also get their turn.

3: it creates among employees a feeling of content with the existing conditions of work and employment.

4: It increases interest in acquiring higher qualifications, in training and in self-development with a view to meet the requirements of promotions.

5: Promotion improve employee morale and job satisfaction

Benefit 6: Ultimately it improves organisational health.

Principles of promotion

Every organisations has to specify clearly its policy regarding promotion based on its corporate policy.

The basic characteristics of a systematic Promotion policy are:

Policy 1: It Should be consistent in the sense that policy should be applied uniformly to all employees irrespective of the background of the persons.

Policy 2: It should be fair and impartial. In other words, it should not give room for nepotism, favoritism etc.,

Policy 3: Systematic line of promotion channel should be incorporated.

Policy 4: It should provide equal opportunities for promotion in all categories of jobs, departments and regions of an organisation.

Policy 5: It should ensure open policy in the same that every eligible employee should be considered for promotion rather than a closed system which considers only a class of employee.

Policy 6: It should contain clear cut norms and criteria for judging merit, length of service, potentiality etc.

Policy 7: Appropriate authority should be entrusted with the task of making a final decision.

Policy 8: Favoritism should not be taken as a basis for promotion.

Problem of Promotion

Promotion benefits the employees and the organisation, it creates certain problems.

- Promotion Disappointments some employee
- Some employee refuse promotion

Promotion Disappointments some employee

Some employees who are not promoted will be disappointed when their colleagues with similar qualifications and experience are .promoted either due to favoritism or due to the lack of systematic promotion policy.

Some employee refuse promotion

There is a general tendency that an employee accepts promotion. But there are several incidents where employees refuse promotions.

These incidents include promotion together with transfer to an unwanted place, promotion to that level where the employee feels that he will be quite incompetent to carry out the job, delegation of unwanted responsibilities and when trade union leaders feel that promotion causes damage to their position in the trade union.

Transfer

It is a form of internal mobility, in which the employee is shifted from one job to another usually at a different location, department, or unit. Transfer can either be temporary or permanent depending on the decision of the organization, and it is initiated by any of the two, i.e. employer or employee.

Employee Transfer is the process of horizontal movement of an employee, wherein there is a change in the job, without any changes or revision in the remuneration, pay, and modification of responsibilities. It is a form of internal mobility, in which the employee is shifted from one job to another usually at a different location, department, or unit.

Transfer can either be temporary or permanent depending on the decision of the organization, and it is initiated by any of the two, i.e. employer or employee. Sometimes, it also includes promotion, demotion or even no change in the status and responsibility.

Purposes of Transfer of Employees

These are the purposes of transfer of employees in HRM:

1. To Meet the Organizational Requirements
2. To Meet Employees' Requests

3. To Ensure Better Utilization of the Employees
4. To Make the Employees More Versatile
5. To Adjust the Workforce
6. To Provide Relief to the Employee
7. To Reduce Conflicts and Incompatibilities
8. To Penalise the Employees
9. To Maintain a Tenure System
10. To Accommodate Family-Related Issues

Types of Transfer in HRM

Let's discussed the types of transfer in HRM:

1. Production Transfers
2. Replacement Transfers
3. Versatility Transfers
4. Shift Transfers
5. Remedial Transfers
6. Precautionary Transfers
7. Sectional Transfers
8. Departmental Transfers
9. Inter-Plant Transfers

Production Transfer

Production transfer is usually practised to prevent lay-off that is to say when there is a surplus of the workforce in the factory, excess workers are laid off. But, if they are transferred to another factory or plant, where there is a shortage of labour, the massive layoff can be.

Replacement transfer

Replacement transfers are transfers in which a long-service employee is transferred to a similar job where he replaces or "bumps" an employee with shorter service. This type of transfer is made when all operations are declining, but management wants to retain the long-service employee as long as possible.

Versatility Transfers

The versatility transfer (better called 'rotation') is for the purpose of providing management with a more versatile group of employees. This type of transfer will increase the versatility of the employee by shifting him from one job to another. The employee gets an opportunity for varied job experience.

Shift Transfer

The act of an employee being moved, upon the initiation of the department, from one unit/shift to another unit/shift.

Remedial Transfer –

It involves movement of an employee within an organization to correct a wrong placement.

Precautionary Transfer

Such transfers are made as a precautionary measure to avoid the misuse of office or misappropriation of funds by the employees.

Sectional Transfer

If a transfer is from one department to another, it is known as departmental transfer. If a transfer is made within the department, such a transfer is known as sectional transfer.

Departmental Transfer

Inter-departmental transfers are necessary when one department performs a service for or funds the activity of another department. Work orders are used to process the transfers between the departments. Sometimes both departments will complete a work order for the transfer.

Inter-Plant Transfer

A transaction to move inventory from one storage bin to another. Depository transfer check (DTC). Check made out directly by a local bank to a particular firm

Types of Transfer in HRM

On the Basis of Purpose

Production Transfers

A shortage or surplus of the workforce is common in different departments in a plant or several plants in an organization. Surplus employees in a department have to be laid off unless they are transferred to another department. Transfers affected to avoid such inevitable layoffs are called production transfers.

Replacement Transfers

A replacement transfer is the transfer of a senior employee to replace the junior employee or a new employee, when the latter is laid off or shifted to another job, Sometimes, it is a temporary arrangement to make use of the services of the senior personnel.

Versatility Transfers

Versatility transfers are effected to make employees versatile and competent in more than one skill. It aims at giving training to the employees of various jobs of similar nature having different operations. It helps the employees to get themselves prepared for promotions and also helps the employer in developing the effective manpower prepared to handle the higher openings.

Shift Transfers

When the unit runs in shifts, employees are transferred from one shift to another on similar jobs. In some undertakings, where shifts are operated regularly, employees may be recruited permanently for the shift, but in some cases, they are rotated from one shift to another as a matter of practice because many employees dislike second or third shift assignment as it interferes with their social or family engagements.

Remedial Transfers

Remedial transfers are effected at the request of the employees and are, therefore, called personal transfers. Personal transfers take place because the initial placement of an employee may have been faulty or the worker may not get along with his supervisor or with other workers in the department.

He may be getting too old to continue his regular job or working conditions may not be well adapted to his personal health. If the job is repetitive, the employee may stagnate and would benefit by transferring to a different kind of work.

Precautionary Transfers

Such transfers are made as a precautionary measure to avoid the misuse of office or misappropriation of funds by the employees. In some undertakings, there are more chances of misuse of office or misappropriation of funds than in others. Generally, it is mentioned in the transfer policy of the organization that an employee cannot stay at one post for more than 3 years or so.

On the Basis of Unit

Sectional Transfers

These transfers are made within the department from one section to another. The main purpose of such transfers may be to train the workers and prepare them to handle the operations of different sections of the department.

Departmental Transfers

Transfers from one department to another department within the plant is called departmental transfer. Such transfers are made if the nature of work is the same or substantially the same in both the departments such as clerical or routine jobs.

Inter-Plant Transfers

If there is more than one plant under the control of the same management, the transfer may be made from one plant to another for varied reasons. Such transfers are called inter-plant transfers.

Causes of Transfer in HRM

In modern organizations, these are the causes of transfer in hrm:

1. Meeting Organizational Needs
2. Meeting Employee's Requests
3. Better Utilization of the Employees
4. Developing All-Rounder
5. Manpower Adjustment
6. Avoidance of Conflicts
7. Punishing the Employees
8. Relief to Employees
9. Tenure System

Causes of Transfer in HRM

Meeting Organizational Needs

A company may transfer employees due to changes in the volume of production, technology, production schedule, product line in organization structure, market conditions, etc. filling in the vacancies which may occur because of separations or because of the need for suitable adjustment in business operations. In short, the purpose of the transfer is to stabilize employment in the organization.

Meeting Employee's Requests

Transfers are also done at the request of the employees. Employees may need transfers in order to satisfy their desire to work under a different superior in a department/ region where opportunities for advancement are bright, in or near their native place, doing a job where the work itself is challenging, etc. Many employees seek transfer because of family-related issues such as marriage or illness.

Better Utilization of the Employees

An employee may be transferred because the management feels that he is not performing satisfactorily and adequately and when the management feels that he may be more useful or suitable elsewhere, where his capacities would be better utilized.

Developing All-Rounder

The employees may be transferred to different jobs to widen their knowledge and skills. In some companies, transfers are made as a matter of policy after an employee has stayed on a job for a specified period. Such rotation from one job to another serves as a tool for developing versatile workers.

Manpower Adjustment

The employees may be transferred from a plant where there is less work to a plant where there is more work. Thus, the employees who have been in service of an organization are not thrown out of employment but adjusted elsewhere.

Avoidance of Conflicts

Where employees find it difficult to get along with colleagues in a particular section or department, they could be shifted to another place to reduce conflict.

Punishing the Employees

Transfers may be made as a disciplinary measure. The employees indulging in undesirable activities may be transferred to remote, far-flung areas or transferred to less important jobs.

Relief to Employees

Transfers may be made to give relief to employees who are overburdened or doing hazardous jobs for long periods. The transfer may also be made to break the monopoly of the employee. The climate of a place may be unsuitable for an employee's health. He may request a transfer to another place, on health grounds.

Tenure System

In senior administrative services of the Government and also in industries, the employees hold certain jobs for a fixed tenure. They are made to move from job to job with a view to acquire a variety of experience and skills and also to ensure

Transfer Policy

A sound, just and impartial transfer policy should be evolved in the organization to govern all types of transfers. This policy should be clearly specified so that the superiors cannot transfer their subordinates arbitrarily and the subordinates may not request transfers even for petty issues.

The management must frame a policy on transfers and apply it to all the transfers instead of treating each case on its merit. Such a policy must be based on the following principles:

1. Transfer policy must be in writing and be made known to all the employees of the organization.
2. The policy must very clearly specify the type and the circumstances under which company-initiated transfers will be made.
3. The basis for transfer should be clearly mentioned in the policy. Whether it will be based on seniority or on skill and competence or any other factor.
4. It should indicate the executive who will be responsible for initiating and approving the transfers.
5. The policy should specify the region or unit of the organization within which transfers will be administered.
6. The effect of the transfer on the pay and seniority of the transferred employee may be clearly evaluated.
7. It should be prescribed in the policy whether training or retraining is required for the new job.
8. Transfers should be clearly defined as temporary or permanent.
9. The interests of the organization are not to be forgotten in framing a policy of transfer.
10. Reasons for mutual transfer of employees or reasons to be considered for personal transfers should be specified.
11. The fact of transfer should be intimated to the person concerned well in advance.
12. Transfers should not be made frequent and not for the sake of transfer only.

Generally, line managers administer the transfers, and personnel managers assist the line managers in this respect.

Difference Between Transfer and Promotion

Let's discussed the difference between transfer and promotion given below:

Transfer	Promotion
It refers to a lateral shift of an individual from one job position to another on the same occupational level and pays scale.	It implies the upward elevation of an individual in terms of job responsibilities, pay scale, and status.

Consideration of merit and seniority does not affect transfer decisions. The incentive value of the transfer is low.	It represents a recognition of and rewards for merit, good performance and behaviour, length of service, commitment, and so on.
It is a routine administrative matter.	It involves thoughtful managerial decisions.
In the case of transfers, outsiders do not enter into consideration.	In promotion management can fill the positions internally or through external selection.
The criteria for transfer may be improving the versatility of employees, rectification or correction of wrong placement, increase or decrease in volume of activity, and punishment for poor performance.	The criteria for promotion may be merit in the performance of the job, the potential for assuming higher responsibilities, and length of service in a job.
Transfers may be multi-directional and reversible.	Normally once an employee is promoted to a higher position, he is not reverted back or demoted to an earlier position.

Transfer of employees

A transfer is a change in job where the new job is substantially equal to the old in terms of pay, status, and responsibilities.

Transfer in HRM?

Transfer means shifting of an employee from one job to another, one unit to another, or one shift to another and may involve a new geographical location. Transfers have a number of objectives, such as moving employees to positions with a higher priority in terms of goals, placing employees in positions more appropriate to their interests or abilities, or filing department vacancies with employees from overstaffed departments.

A transfer involves the shifting of an employee from one job to another without special reference to changing responsibility or compensation. The transfer may involve promotion, demotion, or no change in status and responsibility. By Dale Yoder

Purposes of the transfer of employees

Following are the purposes of the transfer of employees in HRM:

1. To Meet the Organizational Requirements
2. To Meet Employees' Requests
3. To Ensure Better Utilization of the Employees
4. To Make the Employees More Versatile

5. To Adjust the Workforce
6. To Provide Relief to the Employee
7. To Reduce Conflicts and Incompatibilities
8. To Penalise the Employees
9. To Maintain a Tenure System
10. To Accommodate Family-Related Issues.

Types of transfer

Types of Transfer in HRM:

1. Production Transfers
2. Replacement Transfers
3. Versatility Transfers
4. Shift Transfers
5. Remedial Transfers
6. Precautionary Transfers
7. Sectional Transfers
8. Departmental Transfers

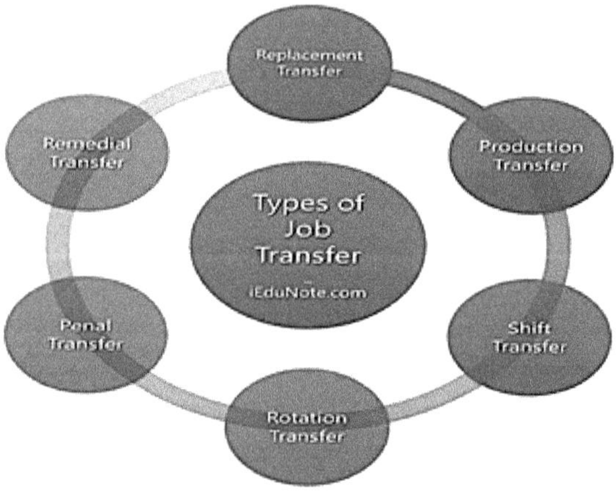

9. Inter-Plant Transfers.

Objectives of Transfer of Employees in a Company:

1. To meet the exigencies of the company's business.
2. To meet the request of an employee.
3. To correct incompatibilities of employee relations.
4. To suit the age and health of an employee.

5. To provide creative opportunities to deserving employees.
6. To train the employee for later advancement and promotion. This involves actually job rotation.
7. To deal with fluctuations in work requirements or exigencies at work, such as situations when there is slackness in the work in one department and an overload of work in another, an employee from the first department may be temporarily transferred to the other department as found necessary.
8. To correct erroneous placement.
9. To place the employee in another department where he/she would be more suitable.

Transfer in HRM - Purpose

Transfers are generally effected to build up a more satisfactory work team and to achieve the following purposes:

(a) To Meet an Employee's Own-request, when he feels uncomfortable on the job because of his dislike of his boss, or his fellow workers, or because better opportunities for his future advancement do not exist there, or because of family Circumstances which may compel him to change the place of his residence. Such transfers generally have their rot in faulty selection and erroneous placement, and are known as personal transfers. They enable employees to feel at home in the work of their choice.

(b) To Utilise Properly the Services of an Employee, when he is not performing satisfactorily and adequately and when the management feels that he may be more useful or suitable elsewhere, where his capacities would be better utilised. Such transfers are called remedial transfers. They act as a follow-up measure of the selection-and- placement procedure and help employees to adjust themselves to suitable jobs.

(c) To Satisfy Such Needs of an Organisation, as may arise out of change in the quantity of promotion, fluctuations in work requirements, and changes in the organisational structure; the introduction of new lines of promotion, the dropping of existing product lines, the reallocation of, or reduction in the work force due to a shortage or a surplus in same section so that lay-offs may be avoided; filling in of the vacancies which may occur because of separations or because of the need for suitable adjustments in business operations.

Such transfers are known as promotion transfers, flexibility transfers, or organisational transfers. The purpose of such transfers is to stabilise employment in an organisation. They are generally controlled centrally through and by the personnel department.

(d) To Increase the Versatility of the Employee, by shifting him from one job to another so that he may have ample opportunities for gaining a varied and broader experience of work. Such transfers are known as versatility transfers. They make it possible for an employee to enjoy the facility of job enrichment, which in turn gives to the management a more effective and experienced employee for a higher job.

(e) To Adjust the Work Force of One Plant with that of another, particularly when one is closed down for reasons beyond the control of the employer. Such transfers are known as plant transfers and are generally effected on humanitarian grounds to ensure that persons who have been long in service of an organisation are not thrown out of employment.

(f) To Penalise the Employee Transfers are Also Done, under which either a difficult trade union activist or intriguer or sea lawyer may be transferred to a remote branch or office where he cannot continue his activities. In Government organisations, this practice is widespread, and is also preferred by the employee to the grim alternative of disciplinary action.

(g) To Help Employees Work, according to their convenience so far as timings are concerned; for example, an employee is transferred from night shift to morning shift or from the first to the second shift (as in the case of women workers who may like to look after their children and do the necessary domestic work in the morning hours). Such transfers are known as shift transfers.

(h) Transfer for the Maintenance of a Tenure System, in senior administrative services of the Government and also in industries, or where there is a system of annual intake of management trainees such transfers are common. Here the employee holds a certain job for a fixed tenure but he is made to move from job to job with a view to enabling him to acquire a variety of experience and skills and also to ensure that he does not get involved in politicking informal groups.

(i) To Replace a New Employee by An Employee, who has been in the organisation for a sufficiently long time. Such transfers are known as replacement transfers, the purpose being to give some relief to an old employee from the heavy presser of work.

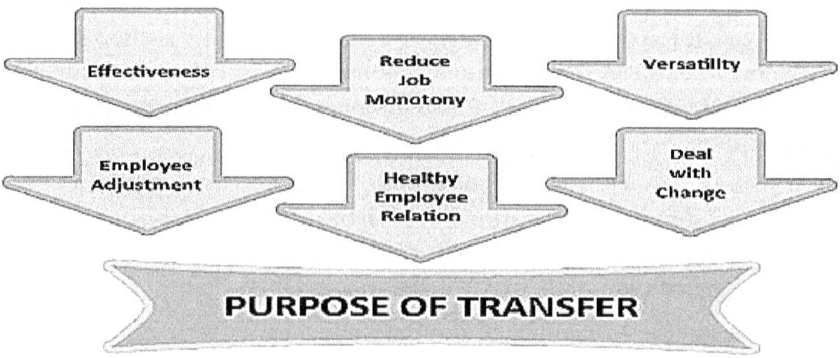

Unit IV

MINIMUM WAGES ACT, 1948

Introduction

Labour laws in India consist of significant legislations such as the Industrial Dispute Act, 1947, Payment of Bonus Act, 1965, Workmen Compensation Act, 1923, Minimum Wages Act, 1948, etc. In the Indian Constitution, labour laws fall under the Concurrent List, which gives power to both Central and state governments to legislate and make rules on the matter. These legislations play significant roles in protecting the rights and interests of the workers, providing employment opportunities to the workers, protecting employees from exploitation, creating a healthy work environment, etc.

The system of paying minimum wages to the employees has been globally accepted as a system to combat poverty and stabilise the economy. The Minimum Wages Act, 1948 was brought into force by the Parliament of India in order to provide due remuneration to the workers and to prevent unfair exploitation of the workers by the employers. The Act lays down the minimum rates of wages and fixing of minimum wage rates for both skilled and unskilled labour and aims to provide a decent standard of living for them. The Act grants power to both the Central and state governments to regulate, review and revise the rate of minimum wages paid to the employees employed in the scheduled employment under their respective jurisdiction. The Act does not discriminate between men and women, it pays all the employees equally for doing the same work.

Understanding the term minimum wage

The International Labour Organisation (ILO) has defined the term minimum wage as the lowest amount of remuneration that an employer is required to pay wage earners for the work performed during a given period, that cannot be reduced by collective agreement or an individual contract. Around 90 member states of the ILO follow the provision of minimum wage.

The purpose of minimum wage is to protect the workers from unduly low pay. It enables them to earn adequate wages for the work done by them and to maintain a minimum living standard. It also acts as a tool to eradicate poverty and to remove discrimination between men and women. This system has been designed and developed in a way to supplement and reinforce other social and employment policies, including collective bargaining, which is used to set terms of employment and working conditions.

In India payment of minimum wages is regulated and administered by the Minimum Wages Act, 1948. Since, India offers one of the most competitive labour costs in Asia, with the national-level minimum wage at around INR 176 which amounts to INR 4576 in a month. However, it is the national-level wage which will vary considering the geographical location and other relevant factors. In India, a complex method of setting a minimum wage is used which defines nearly 2,000 different types of jobs for unskilled workers and over 400 categories of employment which provides a minimum daily wage for each type of job.

Types of wages

In 1948 a tripartite committee, known as the 'Committee on Fair Wages' was established. The committee's report was the benchmark for the formulation of wage policy in India. The committee not only set guidelines for wage rates in the country but also laid down three kinds of wages namely:

1. **Minimum wage:** This is the type of wage provided for bare subsistence so that the workers can maintain a decent standard of living such as providing for education, medical requirements and an adequate level of comfort.
2. **Fair wage:** Any wage paid to the employees that are more than the minimum wage is known as a fair wage. It is the wage that seeks to maintain a level of employment in the industry and also looks after the industry's capacity to pay sufficient remuneration to the employees.
3. **Living wage:** A living wage not only meets the minimum requirement of the employees provided by the employers but also allows individuals or families to afford adequate shelter, food, and other necessities. It also includes health, sanity, education, dignity, comfort, and provide for any contingency.

Need for a meaningful minimum wage

In India, the minimum wages fixed for the labourers are so low that it is not enough even for two meals a day, leave aside the needs of health, education and shelter. The main objective behind minimum wages of the workers should be primarily because of two reasons:

- **Social objective:** Minimum wage is essential for abolishing poverty by providing a basic standard of living to the employees.
- **Economic objective:** The rate of minimum wage should be fixed in such a way that would motivate the workers to put in maximum efforts at their

jobs and thus improve the economy of the country and their standard of living.

Minimum wage legislation in India requires the active support of workers, trade unions, and labour associations. It would also require sincerity on part of the labour departments in each state in order to determine the minimum wage rate on the basis of ethical and humanitarian concerns to ensure basic subsistence for workers in unorganised sectors. Ignorance and illiteracy are also the primary reasons for the exploitation of the employees in the unorganised sectors. Trade unions and NGOs can help by making the workers aware of the legal provisions of the minimum wage rate and the benefits to which they are entitled.

Furthermore, minimum wage data is not readily available to the general public. Only limited official data is available from the National Labour Ministry website which may or may not be updated regularly and in a timely manner. The information available does not permit extensive comparison of wages in formal and informal sectors due to different formats of reporting or recording of wage rates in each state.

Need for Minimum Wages Act, 1948

The Minimum Wages Act, 1948 was enacted by the Indian Legislature to deal with matters relating to providing the minimum wage to the workers so that they can afford their basic needs and maintain a decent standard of livelihood. The Act further ensures a secure and adequate living wage for all labourers and it also guarantees that an employee earns enough to provide for his family. The Act authorises both Central and state governments in fixing the rate of minimum wage. The Minimum Wages Act, 1948 has also laid down a provision for revision of minimum wages in order to cope with the changing prices of basic commodities.

The Act seeks to provide better protection of the rights of the employees by establishing advisory boards to resolve any dispute between the employer and employee regarding the payment of minimum wage to the employees. The Act further appoints a Commissioner for Workmen's Compensation or any other officer of the Central Government exercising functions as a Labour Commissioner for any region, with an experience as a judge in order to hear and decide cases concerning non-payment or payment of less than the minimum wages to the employees. The Act also states provisions for penalising any employer who fails to provide the minimum wage to the employer and contravenes any rule or order made under the Act.

Thereby, it can be said that the enactment of this Act was extremely crucial since it aims to expand the concept of social justice to the workers of scheduled employment and also provide them with the rates of minimum wages fixed by the statute. It also protects the rights and interests of the workers and prevents the workers from being wrongfully exploited by their employers.

Objectives of Minimum Wages Act

The significance of the Minimum Wages Act, 1948 is mentioned below:

1. To fix the minimum rates of wages that are to be provided to the employees and revise such rates of wages every five years.
2. To secure an adequate living wage for all the labourers in the interest of the public.
3. To fix the daily working hours of the employees.
4. To prevent exploitation of the workers by the employers.
5. To ensure that the labourers can maintain a decent standard of living.
6. To provide basic physical needs, good health and a level of comfort to the employees.
7. To penalise the employers when they fail to provide minimum wages to the workers.
8. To establish advisory boards to regulate and administer the provisions of the Act.
9. To lay down the powers and duties of the inspectors for the purposes of this Act.
10. To prevent any employer from wrongfully infringing the right of any employees.
11. To establish appropriate authorities where the employees can seek redressal when the employer has failed to pay the daily wage.
12. To authorise the Central and state governments to make rules and regulations for the purposes of this Act.

Application of Minimum Wages Act

The Minimum Wages Act, 1948 is applicable to the whole of India as laid down in Section 1 of the Act. It applies to any employment if it employs 1000 employees in the respective state. However, it does not apply to any employees in any undertaking owned by the Central Government or of the federal railway, except with the consent of the Central Government.

Essential provisions under Minimum Wages Act

The significant provisions of the Minimum Wages Act, 1948 are mentioned below.

Minimum rates of wages

Under Section 3 of the Act, the minimum wages payable to the employees are to be fixed by the appropriate government. However, this Section also mentions that the rate of wages shall be revised every five years. The appropriate government may fix:

1. The minimum rate of wages for time work,
2. the minimum rate of wage for piece work,
3. a minimum rate of remuneration to apply in the case of employees employed on piece work for the purpose of securing to such employees a minimum rate of wages on a time work basis,
4. a minimum rate of wage to substitute the for the minimum rate which would otherwise be applicable, in respect of overtime work done by employees.

In fixing or revising minimum wages under Section 3 of the Act:

1. Different minimum rates of wages may be fixed for; different classes of work, different scheduled employment, different localities, different age groups, etc.
2. Minimum wages may be fixed by the wage period such as; by the hour, by the day, etc.

Section 4 of the Minimum Wages Act, 1948 states that the minimum wages fixed by the appropriate government must consist of:

1. A basic rate of wages and a special allowance must be adjusted at necessary intervals by the appropriate government to match the cost of living of the employees.
2. The cost of living allowance and the cash value of the concessions in respect of supplies of essential commodities must be computed by a competent authority and at such intervals specified by the appropriate government.

Section 5 states that in order to fix or revise the minimum wage of the employees the appropriate government may establish as many committees and subcommittees necessary to hold enquiries in matters regarding fixing and revision of minimum wage. Further, the appropriate government by notification to the Official Gazette publish its proposal for the information of the individuals who are likely to be affected by such information and thereby specify the date which must not be less than two months from the date of notification of the proposals that will be taken into consideration.

Advisory board

Under Section 7 the appropriate government must appoint advisory boards for coordinating the work of the committees and subcommittees mentioned in Section 5 and also for advising the appropriate government generally in the matter of fixing and revising minimum rates of wages.

Central Advisory Board

In the matters of fixation and revision of minimum rates of wages of the employees, the Central Government shall appoint a Central Advisory Board. The Central Advisory Board shall consist of:

1. Members to be nominated by the Central Government representing employers and employees in the scheduled employment, who shall be equal in number, and
2. Independent persons not exceeding one-third of its total number of members. One such member shall be appointed as the Chairperson by the Central Advisory Board.

Committees

Section 9 of the Act states that the members of committees, sub-committees, and Advisory Boards shall be appointed by the appropriate government. Individuals who are appointed to these committees shall be representatives of employers and employees in scheduled employments and shall be equal in number. The appropriate government shall appoint such an independent person to be the Chairman of the committee.

Wages in kind under the Act

Section 11 of the Minimum wages Act, 1948 mentions how the wages will be payable to the employees.

1. Minimum wages under this Act shall be paid in cash.
2. The appropriate government under necessary circumstances by notification to the Official Gazette authorise the payment of the minimum wages either wholly or partly in kind.
3. The appropriate government by notification to the Official Gazette authorised a provision for the supply of essential commodities at concession rates.
4. The cash value of wages and the concession rates shall be authorised in the prescribed manner stated under the Act.

The payment of wages to the employees under this Act should be done in accordance with Section 12 of the Act, which states that the employer shall pay the minimum rate of wages fixed to every employee working under him within such time and manner prescribed under the Act.

Fixing hours for a normal working day

Section 13 specifies that the appropriate government may:

1. Fix the working hours of a normal day including one or more specified intervals.
2. Provide a day of rest in every period of seven days to all the employees or a class of employees, and adequate remuneration must be provided to the employees during the day of rest.
3. Provide payment to the employees on the day rest which shall not be less than the overtime rate.

When an employee works more than the specified number of hours constituting a normal working day, the employer shall be liable to pay him for every hour or part of the hour at the overtime rate fixed under this Act or under any law of the appropriate government for the time being in force.

Furthermore, under Section 15 if an employee has worked less than the required number of hours constituting a normal working day they shall be entitled to receive wages in accordance with work done by him on that day as if he has worked a full day. However, he might not receive the wages of a full day under certain circumstances.

Maintenance of registers and records

Under Section 18 of the Minimum Wages Act, 1948 every employer will be liable to maintain registers and records relating to the number of employees employed under him, the work done by them, the wages paid to them, the work performed by them, maintain the receipts given by the employers and any other relevant information.

Inspectors

In this Act, the appropriate government by notification to the official gazette shall appoint inspectors in a manner prescribed under the Act. The inspectors shall be liable to exercise their functions within the local limits of their jurisdiction.

1. The inspectors shall enter the premises or places within the local limits of their jurisdiction where the employees are employed to work in respect of which minimum rates of wages have been fixed under this Act, for the purpose of examining the register, record of wages, etc.
2. To examine any person on the premises or places who is an employee.
3. Seize or take copies of registers, records of wages, or other required documents under this act which he may consider relevant in case of commission of any offence.

4. The inspector will be required to exercise any other power as may be prescribed under the Act.

Every inspector under this Act will be deemed to be a public servant within the meaning of the Indian Penal Code,1860.

Claims

The appropriate government may by notification to the Official Gazette appoint any Commissioner for Workmen's Compensation or any officer of the Central Government exercising functions as a Labour Commissioner for any region, with an experience as a judge to hear and decide cases in a particular region about matters relating to non-payment or payment of less than the minimum wages to the employees.

When an application under Section 20 of the Minimum Wages Act, 1948 is made to the authority, the authority shall give adequate opportunities of being heard to both the applicant and the employer. Under this Section, every direction of the authority shall be binding and final. The authority appointed under the Act shall have the powers of a civil court under the Code of Civil Procedure, 1908 for the purposes of taking evidence, enforcing the attendance of witnesses, production of documents, etc.

Procedure before the authority

The procedure before the authority in the matters relating to non-payment or payment of less than the minimum wages to the employees shall take place in the following manner as prescribed under the Act.

- The prescribed authority shall give adequate opportunities of being heard to the employer, applicant or any other person relevant to the case.
- In case of non-payment of wages, or delay in the payment of wages the authority shall direct the refund of such amount to the applicant of the amount unpaid, or delayed along with the compensation for the damages suffered by the employee.
- No compensation will be awarded to the employee if the authority is satisfied that the delay in payment of wages of the employee was a bona fide error. The authorised person was unable to make the payment even though they exercised due diligence.

Penalties for offences

Section 22 of the Minimum Wages Act, 1948 an employer who fails to provide minimum rates of wages to the employees or contravenes any rule or order made under Section 13 of the Act shall be punished with imprisonment for a term which may extend to six months or fine not less than five hundred rupees or both.

Exemptions of the employers in certain cases

When an employer is accused under this Act and brought before the court he will be exempted from such offence under the following circumstances:

1. The employer has used due diligence in the execution of all the provisions of the Act.
2. The other person has committed the offence without his knowledge, connivance or consent. Then in that case the other will be held liable as if he were the employer and the employer will be discharged.

The power of the Central Government to make rules

Section 29 of the Minimum Wages Act, 1948 authorises the Central Government to make rules by notification to the Official Gazette in matters relating to the term of office of the members, the manner of voting, and the mode of conducting business by the Central Advisory Board, and other relevant matters.

The rules made by the Central Government must be laid before the Parliament while it is in session for a total period of thirty days which may consist of one session or two successive sessions.

Furthermore, Section 30 of the Act also authorises the state government to make rules by notification to the Official Gazette for carrying out the purposes of this Act.

Constitutional validity of Minimum Wages Act

The constitutional validity of this Act was challenged before the court in various cases. However, the judiciary played a critical role in determining that the Act was constitutionally valid and it protects the interests of the workers so that they have access to food, shelter, clothing, education, medical assistance, etc. The judiciary also stated that failure to pay below the minimum wage rate amounts to forced labour.

Not violative of Article 19 of the Constitution

The constitutional validity of the Minimum Wages Act, 1948 was first challenged in the case, Bijay Cotton Mills Ltd. v. The State of Ajmer, 1954. In this case, there was an industrial question between the industry and the workers regarding the improvement of wages. The company alleged before the court that the provisions of the Act are illegal since it puts unreasonable restrictions on the employer as he is deterred from resuming his trade or business unless he is ready to pay the minimum wages to the workers. The rights of the employees are also limited, as they are disabled from working in any trade or industry unless the terms are agreed to between them and their employers. Therefore, the Act is violative of Article 19(1)(g) of the Indian Constitution which guarantees freedom of trade and business. However, the Supreme Court of India held that the provisions of the Act are not unreasonable and permissible under Article 19 of the Indian Constitution, moreover, the provisions of the Act have been imposed for the benefit of the general public as the Directive Principles of State Policy embodied under Article 43 of the Constitution.

Thus, it can be said that because of certain provisions of the Act the employers might find it difficult to carry on or start a business, but it is done in order to protect the general interest of the public and so the Act can not be deemed unreasonable or stuck down on such grounds.

Similarly, in the case Bhikusa Yamasa Kshatriya v. Sangamner Akola Bidi Kamgar Union, 1958, the Bombay High Court held that the constitution of the committees and the Advisory Boards under the Minimum Wages Act, 1948 did not contravene the statutory provisions of the prescribed legislature and further on careful examination of the Act it was noticed that Section 3(3)(iv) of the Act does not contravene Article 19(1) of the Indian Constitution neither does it violate equal protection of the law guaranteed by the Constitution.

Not violative of Article 14 of the Constitution

Furthermore, the Act is not violative of Article 14 of the Constitution which states equality before the law. It was brought into light by India's Union Labour and Employment Minister Shri Mallikarjuna Kharage that the variation of minimum wages of workers in different states is due to the different socio-economic conditions, prices of commodities, paying capacity, productivity, etc. which impacts the wage rate paid to the workers in a particular state. In the case, N.M. Wadia Charitable Hospital v. State of Maharashtra, 1986, it was held by the Bombay High Court that fixing different rates of minimum wages for different localities is permitted under the Constitution and the labour laws of the country, thus fixing different rates of minimum wages for different areas is not discriminatory and not violative of the Constitution.

MGNREGA wages rate or minimum wages rate

Mahatma Gandhi National Rural Employment Guarantee Act is a scheme which guarantees employment for 100 days at a rate of wage of INR 120 per day that came into force in 2009. The Act is applicable to everyone whether they are below the poverty line or above. The Central Government removed the MNREGA wage rates from the state's lowest minimum wage rates in January 2009 when states such as Uttar Pradesh, Rajasthan and Maharashtra revised and increased their minimum wage rates. This had serious consequences across the nation for the MNREGA scheme directly in the Central Government budget. Protests began in various parts of the country concerning workers' welfare, poor payments, unclear sources of funds, etc.

The National Advisory Council recommended that MGNREGA wage rates should be coordinated with the minimum wage rates, but this was rejected by the Central Government. The Central Government stuck on its decision to freeze MGNREGA wages even after a Supreme Court order. Eventually, the Prime Minister agreed to accept the recommendations and converted MNREGA wages into minimum wage rates until an expert committee produced a desired inbox.

An overview on Workmen compensation Act 1923

The Workmen Compensation Act, 1923 is an enactment that was issued by the tral Government and was implemented by various State Governments which gives social security to workers. This security is offered by the law for people who work.

The Act was formed after it was noted that laborers were getting more exposed to danger with the use of advanced and sophisticated machinery. The common law had it that the employer would only take up the compensation responsibility if it is found that the industrial accident was a result of his negligence. In India, the issue of compensating workmen after fatal and major accidents hit the road in 1884. It was then in 1885 that the factory and mining inspectors realized that the Fatal Accidents Act, 1885, was not enough to attend to the intended purposes.

The State offered a hearing ear when members of the Legislative Assembly, employers' representatives, workers and experts in medicine and insurance formed a committee that gave a report that led to the enacting of the Workmen's Compensation Act in 1923.

The passing of the Act put a stop and offered a relief for workers who would have gone through court processes that are often expensive, an effort to seek compensation whenever they acquired an injury during employment.

Aspects of The Workmen Compensation Act

The Act has its basis on two aspects:

Theory of least cost.

The production cost shall have the cost of blood and workmen included.

For an industry to run, an employer uses capital, skills in business and the labor of workers who are paid for the labor. The management has to put aside finances for the possibility of the expense needed to repair the machines when they break down. If that care and attention can be given to machines, human beings working in the same environment need also receive care and attention for the risks they undertake when working in that industry.

Social security offers to ensure compensation is paid to a disabled or injured person only if the accident rose in the middle of the employment. The compensation paid to a workman by an employer when an accident occurs is a relief and social security measure provided by the Act. A workman is now able to get compensation regardless of his negligence.

The Act also puts in place the amount that is to be paid according to the intensity of the injury. This makes an employer aware of the amount of compensation he is liable to pay in case of an accident.

The Act is recognized all over India and applies to all workmen and casual workers in factories, plantations, mines, transport establishments, railways, ships, circuses, construction work and any other potentially dangerous occupations made mention in Schedule II of this Act. The Act is not applicable to people in the Armed Forces.

Objective of The Workmen Compensation Act

The Workmen's Compensation Act of 1923 was formed majorly to give compensations to workmen in the event of an accident.

The Act has it that employers should have duties and obligations that include the welfare of workers after an injury resulting from employment in the same way they have reserved the right to make profits. The Act aims to see workmen have a sustainable life after an employment-related accident.

The Royal Commission on Labour made note of the following:

The Act also goes further to ensure the prevention of accidents by giving workmen a relief from anxiety and renders the industry more friendly and desirable.

It has become a necessity for workmen to be protected due to the increasing complexity of the industry through the increased use of sophisticated machinery that poses a potential danger to workers and also the possibility of poverty after injury.

The Act tried as much as possible to curb the chances of disputes which has led to events which are arbitrary. However, the general outcome is satisfactory since the merits are more than the demerits when it comes to the welfare of workmen.

Scope of the Act:

The Act is applicable only to those workmen working in industries as specified in the Act. The Act affords protection to a workman from losses or injury caused by accident arising out of and in the course of employment subject to certain exceptions as laid down in the Act.

Employer's Liability for Compensation:

To make the employer pay compensation, the death or injury suffered by the workman must be consequence of an 'accident arising out of and in the course of his employment' is dependent upon the following four conditions:

(1) The casual connection between the injury and the accident (i.e., personal injury is caused to workman while on work);

(2) The injury and accident caused during the course of employment;

(3) The probability tenable to reason that the work contributed to the causing of personal injury; and

(4) The applicant proves that it was the work and the resulting strain which contributed to or aggravated the injury.

1. Applicability of the Act:

The Act is applicable throughout India except the State of Jammu & Kashmir. The Act does not apply to those areas which are covered by the Employees' State Insurance Act, 1948.

2. The salient features of the Act are as follows:

I. Extent and Application:

The Act extends to whole of India. It is also applicable to the workman recruited by companies/establishments registered in India and sent for work abroad.

It applies to:

(a) All railway servants not permanently employed in any administrative, district or sub-divisional office of a railway and not employed in any capacity as is specified in Schedule II to the Act;

(b) Persons employed in any such capacity as is specified in Schedule II to the Act. Schedule II includes persons employed in factories, mines, plantations, mechanically propelled vehicles, construction works and certain other hazardous occupations. In all, there are 48 employments listed in the Schedule; and

(c) Persons employed in employments added to Schedule II by the State Government in exercise of the powers conferred on them under section 2(3) of the Act. In this connection, a statement indicating the additions made so far by different State Governments is enclosed (Annex-I).

There is no wage limit for coverage under the Act. All the employees employed in Scheduled employment including the railway servants men tioned at (a) above, are therefore, covered under the Act.

II. Contingencies in which Compensation is Payable:

Compensation is payable in case of temporary/permanent disablement or death as a result of an employment injury. The contracting of any disease listed in Schedule III to the Act is deemed to be an injury by accident.

III. Occupational Diseases:

If a workman employed in the employment specified in Schedule III of the Act contracts any occupational disease peculiar to that employment he becomes eligible for payment of compensation under the Act.

The occupational diseases should be contracted while in the service of an employer in the specified employment. The Schedule III divides the occupational diseases in three parts, namely Part-A, Part-B and Part-C.

For diseases specified in Part-A, there is no qualifying period of employment. In case of diseases specified in Part-B, a person should have been employed in the specified employment for a continuous period of not less than six months before the disease is contracted.

For the diseases specified in Part-C, the qualifying period is specified by the Central Government. The qualifying period speci fied for the diseases figuring in Part-C of the Schedule is as given below:

(a) Pneumoconioses 7 years

(b) Pagassosis 3 years

(c) Byssionesis 7 years

No qualifying period is required to be specified.

Note:

(1) Where the monthly wages of a workman exceed two thou sand rupees, his monthly wages for the purposes of (a) and (b) above shall be deemed to be two thousand rupees only.

(2) The minimum rates of compensation for permanent disablement and death specified in the Act is rupees Sixty thousand and fifty thousand respectively. The maximum amount of compensation works out to about Rs. 2,74,248.00 for permanent disablement and Rs. 2,28,540.00 for death.

V. Administration:

The Act does not provide for appointment of Inspectors. However, under Section 32 of the Act, the State Governments/Union Territory Admin istrations have to frame rules to carry out the purposes of the Act.

The rule making power under the Act was originally vested in the Central Govern ment and in exercise of these powers, the Workmen's Compensation

Rules, 1924 were framed. Some of the State Governments have subsequently farmed their own rules under the Act.

In this connection, a statement showing the names of the States/UTs, which have so far framed necessary rules under the Act, is attached (Annex-II). The remaining States/UTs are being reminded to expedite the framing of rules under the Act.

VI. Settlement of Claims under the Act:

The claims for compensation broadly fall in three categories, namely (i) uncontested cases of disablement; (ii) disputed cases of disablement and (iii) fatal cases. The procedures for settlement of the three types of cases are as given below:

(i) Uncontested Cases:

(a) After a workman has given notice of the accident, the employer is expected to arrange for medical examination of the workman. It must be free of charge. The medical Examination will indicate the nature of the disablement.

(b) If the disablement is of temporary nature the employer will pay compensation as half monthly payments, direct to the workmen.

(c) If the disablement is of permanent nature compensation will be paid in lump sum by the employer to the workman if he is a male over 18 years of age. In the case of woman and minors, the employer will deposit the amount of compensation with the Com missioner, for disbursement.

(d) Where a workman has agreed to accept and has taken a smaller sum than the amount fixed by the Act his right to bring proceed ings for the balance are protected.

(e) Any agreement with the workman for a lump sum payment must be registered with the Commissioner by the employer.

(ii) Disputed Cases:

(a) If the employer refuses to pay compensation or does not pay the full amount due, the workman has to make an application to the Commissioner for Workman's Compensation appointed by the State Government or Union Territory.

The application has to be made in Form 'F* prescribed under the Workman's Compensation Rules. An illiterate person can have the application prepared under the direction of the Commissioner.

(b) A claim for compensation must be preferred before the Commis sioner within 2 years of the occurrence of the accident or in the case of death within 2 years of the date of death.

In the case of contracting of a disease the accident is deemed to have occurred on the first of the day during which the workman was continuously absent in consequence of the disablement caused by the disease.

(iii) Fatal Cases:

(a) The amount of compensation due has to be deposited by the employer with the Commissioner for Workmen's Compensation. The Act specifically provided that no payment made directly by the employer shall be deemed to be a payment of compensation.

(b) The Commissioner shall distribute the lump sum amount of com pensation to the dependants in such proportion as he may decide.

(c) If the employer does not deposit the compensation the dependant or dependants have to make an application to the Commissioner in Form 'G' prescribed under the Workmen's Compensation Rules for the issue of an order to deposit compensation.

VII. Extension of the provisions of the Workmen's Compensation Act to Hazardous Employments in Agriculture:

The Workmen's Compensation Act, 1923 already applies to workers employed in farming by tractors or other contrivances driven by steam or other mechanical power or electricity etc.

The State Governments of Andhra Pradesh etc. were advised in March, 1976 to consider addition of the following employments to Schedule-II to the Act in accordance with the provision of sub-Section (3) of Section 2 of the Act:

(i) Employed in clearing of jungles or reclaiming land or ponds in which on any one day of the proceeding twelve months more than twenty-five persons have been employed ;

(ii) Employed in cultivation of land or rearing and maintenance of live stock or forest operations or fishing in which on any one day of the proceeding twelve months more than twenty-five persons have been employed ;

(iii) Employed, otherwise than in cleric. I capacity, in installation, main tenance, repair of pumping equipment used for lifting of water from wells, tube-wells, ponds, lakes, stream etc.;

(iv) Employed, otherwise than in clerical capacity, in the construction, boring or deepening of an open well/ dug well through mechanical contrivances;

(v) Employed, otherwise than in clerical capacity in the construction, working, repair or maintenance of a bore well, bore-cum-dug well, fitter point etc.;

(vi) Employed in spraying and dusting of insecticides or persticides in agricultural operation/ or plantations;

(vii) Employed in working or repair of maintenance of bulldozers, tractors, power tillers etc.

As per available information, the State Governments of Andhra Pradesh, Arunachal Pradesh, Assam, Bihar, Haryana, Karnataka, Kerala, Maharashtra, Meghalaya, Orissa, Punjab, Tamil Nadu and Tripura and U.T.

Administrations of Chandigarh, Dadra and Nagar Haveli and Pondicherry have already made the proposed additions with effect from 15.9.95.

The Central Govern ment has included all the above mentioned employments in Schedule II of the Act by amending the Schedule. The matter is not, therefore, being pursued further with the remaining States/UTs.

VIII. Last Amendment of the Act in 1995

(a) The provisions of the Workmen's Compensation Act, 1923, were reviewed by the Law Commission of India (1974) and (1989). The Commission had made a number of recommendations for amend ment of the Act.

Based on their recommendations and suggestions received from the Ministries/ State Governments. The Act has been amended for carrying out certain amendments.

The amendments made by the Workmen's Compensation (Amendment) Act, 1995 provides inter-alia for enhancement in the rate of compensation from 40% to 50% and from 50% to 60% of the monthly wage in the case of death and permanent total disablement respectively;

(b) The minimum rate of compensation for permanent total disable ment and death have been fixed at Rs. 60,000/- and Rs. 50,000/- respectively, as against the previous rates of Rs. 24,000/- and Rs. 20,000/- respectively;

(c) The monthly wage ceiling specified in Explanation II under Sec tion 4(1) for working out the maximum amount of compensation has been enhanced from Rs. 1000/- to Rs. 2000/-. The rate of compensation is linked to the age of the workman at the time of his disablement or death.

The workers getting disabled/dying at an early age are, therefore entitled to compensation at a comparatively higher rate.

(d) A provision for payment of Rs. 1000/- towards funeral expenses has been made in addition to compensation;

(e) The Act has been made applicable to workmen recruited by Companies registered and based in India and sent for work abroad;

(f) Sixteen new employments have been added to Schedule-II. In addition to State Governments, the Central Government has also been empowered to add hazardous employment in Schedule-II.

(g) Three new occupational diseases added to Schedule-Ill. Power to add occupational diseases in Schedule-Ill conferred also on the Central Govt.

(h) The claimant of compensation may have the claim/petition filed/ transferred also before the Commissioner for the area in which the workman ordinarily resides.

Except this all other provisions of the Workmen's Compensation (Amendment) Act, 1995 have been brought into force with effect from 15.9.1995.

Statement showing the names of States which have framed the Rules under the Workmen's Compensation Act, 1923.

1. Pondicherry
2. Uttar Pradesh
3. Tamil Nadu
4. Kerala
5. Andhra Pradesh
6. Sikkim
7. Tripura
8. Rajasthan
9. Himachal Pradesh
10. Goa
11. Dadra & Nagar Haveli
12. Daman and Diu
13. Lakshadweep Andaman & Nicobar Karnataka
16. Maharashtra

Conclusion

The Workman Compensation Act, 1923 was formed to provide compensations for workers who acquired/acquire injuries caused by accidents in the course of employment. It ensure that their rights and value as labourers is maintained. Therefore employers are obligated to pay compensations to workers who got injuries that led to disablement or even death in the course of employment.

Payment of Bonus Act, 1965

Introduction

The payment of bonus is dealt by "Payment of Bonus Act, 1965", read with "payment of Bonus Rules, 1975", (central rules), the main purpose of the enactment is to impose a legal obligation on the employer to provide for payment of bonus.

The Payment of Bonus Act applies to every factory and establishment employing not less than 20 persons on any day during the accounting year.

What is Bonus?

Bonus is considered as "reward" or any additional payment made to their monthly remuneration, given by the employer to the employee in any establishment. The basic objective to give the bonus is to share the profit earned by the organisation amongst the employees.

Any payment made in kind is perquisite, not a bonus.

The Minimum bonus will be provided 8.33% of the salary during the year, or one hundred rupees will be given in case of employees above 15 years and sixty rupees in case of employees below 15 years, whichever is higher. The maximum bonus is 20% of salary during the accounting year.

What are the Establishments/Industries/Factories to which the act is Applicable?

The act is extent to the whole of India, and the act is applicable to

- Every Factory
- Other Establishments where 20 or more persons are employed on any day during the year
- Any Establishment or Class of establishment notified in the Gazette by the Appropriate Government
- Part-time Employees also included.

The Establishments covered under the Act Shall continue to pay the bonus even if the number of employees falls below subsequently.

What are the categories of Establishments to which the Act is not applicable?

- Employees of General Insurance Business or LIC
- Seamen defined under the Merchant Shipping Act
- Employees of RBI
- Employees of Unit Trust of India, IDBI, Deposit Insurance Corporation etc

What are the Eligibility criteria required to be fulfilled by the employees to receive Bonus?

Any person is eligible to receive a bonus under the act, on fulfilment of the following criteria:

- The employee must receive salary/wage up to Rs. 21,000/- per month (By the Amendment of 2015)
- The employee must have worked in the factory or establishment for not less than 30 days in a year

However, on the commission of certain acts, the employee gets disqualified from getting a bonus, such as any frauds, violent behaviour, riots, theft, misappropriation or sabotage of any property. (Section 9 of the Act)

What is the Maximum time for Payment of Bonus?

The bonus shall be paid within 8 months from the end of the accounting year, or within a month from the date of enforcement of the act.

How is the Amount of Bonus payable calculated?

The act prescribes for the minimum bonus, that is 8.33% of the employee's Salary/wages, which is the least percent mandatorily to be paid by every establishment or organisation covered by the act, (Section 10 of the Act); on the other hand, the maximum amount of bonus shall not exceed, 20% of the salary/ wages of the employees (Section 11 of the Act).

The ceiling amount on which the bonus payable is calculated is Rs. 7,000 per month (amendment of 2015), earlier this amount was Rs 3,000. Therefore, if the employee receives Gross Salary up to of Rs 21,000 per month, the employee is eligible to receive bonus.

For bonus calculation only employee's Salary/Wages and Dearness allowance is considered.

Therefore, if the Basic Salary and Dearness Allowance is less than Rs. 7,000 (calculation ceiling), the Bonus will be calculated on the actual amount, and in case the Basic Salary and Dearness Allowance, exceeds Rs. 7,000; bonus will be calculated on Rs 7000 only.

Bonus Calculation:

1. **Basic Salary + DA <7,000, then in such cases,**

   Bonus Payable = (Basic Salary + DA) * Amount %, either 8.33% (establishment is supposed to give even in case of deficit) or could go up to 20%

2. **Basic Salary+ DA >7000, then in such cases,**

   Bonus Payable= Rs. 7000, % either 8.33% (establishment is supposed to give even in case of deficit) or could go up to 20%.

What is the Statutory compliance on the part of Employer?

Considering the Act, there are certain obligations or the compliances on the part of the Employer which they are supposed to comply to, if not, they could be subjected to certain offences or penalties provided in the act.

Several compliances that the employer needs to follow are:

- The employer shall pay the amount of Bonus within 8 months, from the end of the accounting year, in cash
- The employer shall prepare Registers such as:
  - o Register having the entire computation of allocable surplus, in FORM A
  - o Register showing set-on and set-off, in FORM B
  - o Register containing details such as amount of bonus payable, deductions to be made, the amount disbursed, in FROM C
- Employer shall upload details of Annual Returns in FORM D, on the Portal of Ministry of Labour and Employment, on or before 1st day of Feb, every year
- Every employer is supposed to file Annual Return in FROM D, to the inspector on or before 1st Feb every year
- In case of any disputes relating to the payment of bonus, and the case is before any authority, then in such cases, amount shall be paid within 1 month from the date the award passed becomes enforceable.

What are the Offences and Penalties provided by the Act?

- If any person contravenes any provision of the act or rules, then such person shall be punished with "imprisonment" which may extend up to 6 months; or "fine" which may extend up to Rs 1,000; or both
- If any person receives any direction under the Act, and fails to comply with it, such person shall be punished with "imprisonment" which may extend up to 6 months; or "Fine" up to Rs 1000 or both
- In case the offence under the act is committed by the company, then every person responsible for the business of the company (Managing Director, CEO, CFO, Managerial Head), will be punished accordingly

What are the Recent updates/Changes under the Act?

In recent years, there has been an amendment in the year 2015, which is Payment of Bonus (Amendment) Act, 2015, came into force on 1st April 2014, the calculation ceiling for payment of bonus was increased to Rs.7,000.

Furthermore, the Payment of Bonus (Amendment) Rules, 2016 was published in the official gazette, which made an amendment to the central rules of 1975.

Frequently Asked Questions (FAQs)

Does a person under 15 years of age entitled to receive a bonus under the act?

In case the employee has not completed 15 years, in such case, the minimum amount of bonus received by him/her will be Rs. 60/-, and for other employees the minimum bonus amount is Rs 100/-.

How to calculate the number of working days under the Act?

The employee will be considered to work even in the following cases:

- Employee laid off under an agreement
- On paid leave
- Absent due to temporary disablement (caused by accident in course of employment)
- If the employee is on maternity leave

How is gross profit calculated?

In case the of a banking company, it will be calculated in the manner specified in the First Schedule of the Payment of Bonus Act, 1965. In any other case, in the manner specified in Second Schedule of the Payment of Bonus Act, 1965.

What is an Accounting Year? Is it different for different establishments?

- **In case of a Corporation:** The day on which the books and accounts of the corporation is closed and balanced.
- **In case of a Company:** The period for which the profit or loss account of the company is laid before the annual general meeting.
- **In any Other case:** The year commencing from 1st April, or in case the employer closes and balances the accounts of the establishments at any day other than 31st March, then the day on which the Books and Accounts are closed and balanced is considered to be the accounting year.

What is Available surplus and how is it calculated?

Available surplus = gross profit – (depreciation under sec 32 of the Income Tax Act + any amount of development rebate or investment allowance + any direct tax which employer is liable to pay + any other sums specified in third schedule)

Do overtime, HRA, Travel allowances form part of salary in calculating bonus?

No. in calculating bonus, only the Basic Salary and Dearness Allowance are included. Rest HRA, Overtime salary, Travelling Concessions, bonus, Employees Contribution to PF, Gratuity are not considered for Bonus calculation.

Are "Available Surplus" and "Allocable Surplus" two different thing or are the same?

The employer at first calculates his gross profit, and then makes certain deductions specified under section 6 of the Act, after this the amount so received is "Available Surplus". Now from the available surplus, the employer calculates a certain percentage in accordance to sec 2(4), the amount so received is "Allocable Surplus".

If the allocable surplus exceeds the minimum amount of bonus, then in such case what amount shall be paid as bonus?

In case the allocable surplus is more than the amount payable as bonus to the employees as a minimum bonus, then in such case, the employer shall pay bonus on the salary/wage earned by the employee in that year to a maximum 20%

What amount can be deducted from bonus by the employer?

There are certain cases where the employer has the right to make deductions from the amount of bonus payable to the employees, such as

- If employer made any payment of "customary bonus" in the year
- If the employee caused any financial loss to the employer

What is the safeguard provided under the act in case of non-payment of bonus?

If the employee is entitled to receive a bonus under any agreement, award and has not yet received within the due date, then in such cases, the employee has the right to make an application to the central/state govt., and the govt issues certificate to the collector having jurisdiction to recover such amount.

Could there be different rates for payment of bonus for different employees in an establishment?

No. the rates cannot be different, it has to be equal for all the eligible employees. According to the Act, it is supposed to be between 8.33% to 20%. However, the percentage may vary from one accounting year to another, as it depends upon profits earned by the company.

Unit V

EMPLOYEE RELATIONS

Employee relations is a hot-topic buzzword in business circles these days, and for good reason: the relationship between an employer and its employees is an integral part to the longevity of any successful company or organization. But for something so critical to business operations, the details can be irritatingly vague and general.

Vertical and Horizontal Employee Relations

You may hear the terms "vertical and horizontal employee relations" thrown around like dares by the limbo bar at the latest company party, but don't worry: you don't have to break your back to understand them. These terms describe the two main hierarchies in employee relations. All employee relations issues and strategies will involve one, or both, of these groups.

- **Vertical Employee Relations:** This refers to relationships between an employee and his or her superiors (e.g., management, executives, administration).
- **Horizontal Employee Relations:** This term encompasses all same-level employee-to-employee relationships, including employees who are working together on a project or employees who are simply sharing a chat during break time.

10 Examples of Employee Relations Responsibilities

One of the problems with employee relations is that it covers a huge range of topics. After all, "anything involving employees" is a big umbrella. In order to relieve some of your confusion, here are ten common examples of subjects and issues covered by employee relations. It is also worth noting that many of these responsibilities can be easily managed by most of today's recruiting platforms if you feel like you need some technological help.

Encouraging Employee Engagement

Community-building activities, advocacy of a life/work balance, incentives and rewards, professional development opportunities—all of these are some of the things employee relations departments can do to encourage employee engagement and interest. Happy employees work better than dissatisfied ones and a good working environment is great for productivity. Though there are many different approaches out there, from providing different physical environments to organizing holiday events, companies should always strive to keep employees content and healthy.

Improving Workplace Communication

Companies can make or break a good relationship with an employee over the quality of communication. A good employee relations department will continue to try and improve workplace communication, whether that means establishing policies or encouraging transparent exchanges. This applies to communications that happen both at a company-wide scale and at a more personal level—changes in company direction versus performance reviews, for example. It can also apply to communications outside of the company, such as through social media.

Settling Disputes and Conflicts

Unfortunately, it's a fact of life that people will disagree with each other. The more people are involved in the disagreement, the greater the overall discontent, and by extension, the impact on the workplace. In cases such as this, the role of employee relations is to resolve the conflicts before they start to spiral and negatively influence others. This is also true for disputes or issues the employee has with the company.

Addressing Sexual Harassment and Bullying

Employees sexually harassed or bullied (or who witnessed it happening to another individual) should make reports to an employee relations department. The department is then responsible for investigating the allegation, reaching a conclusion and taking any necessary steps to resolve the situation and end the harassment or bullying. Employee relations is also responsible for setting up any preventative measures, such as scheduling anti-harassment courses and writing anti-mistreatment policies.

Overseeing Health and Safety Procedures

An unsafe workplace environment is a recipe for disaster. Injuries, infrastructure damage—all of this can be disastrous to employees and employers. Employee relations must therefore promote awareness of any risks, ensure adequate training where necessary and write company-wide policies in the event of an emergency. Examples include first aid training and fire evacuation procedures.

If an injury or accident does occur, the department is responsible for handling medical leave and compensation.

Handling Wage Concerns

Much like health and safety procedures, the subject of wages—and by extension hours and expectations around compensation or shift work—are handled by an employee relations department. This includes things like attendance, compensation packages, timekeeping and vacation days. Wage disputes, requests for a pay raise and annual reviews or performance bonuses are typically dealt with or communicated by the department. Employee relations is also responsible for ensuring both employees and the company are meeting state and federal wage standards.

Clarifying Company Policy

If an employee has a question about company policy, it is the responsibility of employee relations to provide an answer. They should also address any relevant concerns or comments about the policy, and communicate clearly if the policy is changed or modified.

Conducting Workplace Investigations

Any situation warranting further investigation—such as harassment accusations or allegations of misconduct—will fall under the jurisdiction of an employee relations department. In most cases, the department will conduct these investigations internally, unless it must involve outside parties (e.g., law enforcement). Employee relations will also arrange any measure taken after the conclusion of an investigation, for example, a "recognizing sexual harassment" course.

Communicating With Employee Unions

Employee unions will typically elect a representative responsible for liaising with the company. The company must then find someone internally to liaise with the liaison. This role typically falls to someone in an employee relations department. This relationship is the main point of contact, collaborative or otherwise, between a union and a company, and may involve responsibilities including wage negotiation, employee rights and setting up meetings between unions and upper management.

Monitoring Overall Employee Morale and Performance

In order to evaluate whether initiatives are working, employee relations departments must regularly monitor the morale and performance of employees. By opening up opportunities for reviews and feedback—both anonymous and face-to-face—employee relations can track the company atmosphere and hopefully resolve any brewing negative sentiment before it can grow too far out of control.

Some employee relations departments choose to conduct these reviews in an organized and data-based way, while others (especially smaller organizations) may choose a more conversational approach. The results of these sessions can help employee relations departments choose which areas or problems they should focus on and which current initiatives they should cut or continue.

Importance of Employee Relations

At its most basic, an employee relations department remains important for a very simple reason: without employees, a company could not function. Companies want to keep experienced, productive and valuable employees for as long as possible—an effort often referred to as employee retention. To do this, employees must be happy enough that they will not—or at least will remain less likely to—leave the organization. Enter employee relations.

An organization with a positive relationship between and among management and its employees may see both the retention rates and overall productivity soar. Both of these things have a tangible impact on the company's value and indeed play a key role in determining the success of an organization. Without recognizing and implementing employee relations strategies, many companies would not be able to make it off the ground, much less achieve long-term success.

Commonly Used Employee Relations Strategies

Managing employee relationships is a huge job—even for a fully staffed and well-trained department. Here are some commonly used strategies and ideas for fostering a positive, healthy workplace.

- Encourage cooperation and collaboration. Projects involving multiple departments, teams made up of a mix of employees, regular team meetings, scheduled communal lunch breaks—many strategies can be used to foster a cooperative and collaborative workplace environment.
- Make sure communication is transparent, timely and relevant. Nobody wants to hear from Twitter or a co-worker that a round of layoffs is coming, then wait for a week to pass before a company releases an official statement ... about the new sales product. Make sure communication is precise, straightforward, topical and sensitive to whatever concerns employees might have. Likewise, promote open dialogue between and among employees and supervisors.
- Set and communicate company goals. It can be disconcerting for an employee to be operating in the blind. Knowing what an employee is

working toward can be motivating while receiving invitations to company retreats with no stated purpose can be frustrating. Communicating the reasoning and goals behind actions, plans and initiatives will help employees build trust in the company's mission and encourage loyalty.

- Have appropriate policies in place to reduce conflicts. Much of employee relations is anticipating a problem and setting up a plan to address it well in advance of the problem actually happening. Clear anti-harassment policies with precise definitions, examples and consequences, for example, can help employees to be more mindful in interactions and actions. A defined procedure for wage disputes, on the other hand, can help the dispute be resolved quickly and efficiently.
- Respond quickly and thoroughly to any issue. Whether it's a bullying allegation, a request for a pay raise or a complaint about company policy, it's important to take the situation seriously. Don't make an employee wait for a reply or brush off concerns, as it may make it impossible to gain their trust. It could also affect the company's reputation.
- Provide opportunities for employees to leave feedback. If an employee feels like they're just another cog in a corporate machine with no input about anything that happens, they're more likely to feel dissatisfied. Try to provide regularly scheduled occasions for employees to leave constructive feedback on company direction and policies.
- Offer career advice and professional development. After a few years in the same position, most employees will want to start looking for promotion opportunities—whether at their current company or elsewhere. A good employee relations department will help point employees toward promotions within the company. Similarly, they will regularly provide opportunities for professional development to all employees.
- Celebrate events and holidays. Birthdays, weddings, babies, religious holidays, nondenominational seasonal parties—the list of possible events to celebrate goes on. There's no need to go above and beyond for each event, of course, but small moments of recognition—such as a birthday cake or card—are nice, though be sure to ask any individual before drawing attention to them. Not everyone appreciates the extra attention.
- Plan get-together opportunities outside work. Not every employee will want to interact outside of work, so be careful to ask employees what they'd like to do and don't mandate any extracurricular activities. A good approach is to arrange nonmandatory activities, such as kickball teams or happy hours, and let the people most interested get involved in the organization. This way, interest and community growth can happen organically instead of feeling like just another company-mandated initiative.

- Support a healthy work/life balance for all employees. Employees constantly subjected to last-minute schedule changes, impossible deadlines, overtime-required workloads or inconsistent hours are not employees who will want to stick around.

While the above points are good strategies for improving employee relations, it's important to remember they're also generalized. Any company with a truly successful approach toward employee relations will have customized a strategy to fit the organization. Don't be afraid to try out a few things to see what will stick, but stay flexible when it comes to adjusting policies and plans in order to stay receptive to employee needs and interests.

Characteristics of Industrial Relation

Following are the significant features of industrial relations:Industrial relations are the result of employment relationships in industrial enterprises.Industrial relations introduced the concept and method of balancing and cooperating. Industrial relations formulate rules and regulations to maintain harmonious relations.The intervention of the Government to shape the industrial relation is made through laws, agreements, rules, charters, etc.Industrial relations incorporate both individual relations and collective relations.Several parties play a role in industrial relations. The main parties are employees and their organisation, employers and their association, and government.

Objectives of Industrial Relation

Following are the different objectives of industrial relation."To establish industrial peace.To safeguard the interests of both workers and management. To avoid industrial disputes.To raise the production capacity.To establish industrial democracy.To minimise the labour turnover rate and absenteeism. To safeguard the workers economic and social interests.To contribute to the economic development of the country through productivity.To establish a full employment situation.To minimise strikes, lockout, Heroes, etc., by providing good working conditions and fair wages to the workers.

Nature of Industrial Relation

Industrial relations are concerned with the relationship between management and workers.Industrial relations safeguards the interest of employees.Industrial relations are concerned with the system, rules, and procedures used by unions and employees to determine the reward for effort and other conditions of employment, safeguard the interests of the employees and their employer and regulate how employers treat their employees.Industrial relations maintain a balance with employee expectations, employer associations, trade unions, and other social and economic institutions of societies.Industrial relations help in resolving disputes, conflicts, and controversies between labour and management.

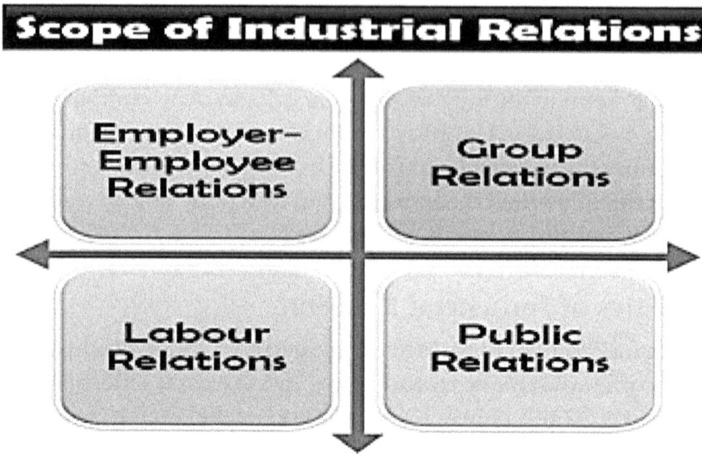

Discipline

Discipline is the regulation and modulation of human activities to produce a controlled performance. The real purpose of discipline is quite simple. It is to encourage employees to confirm to established standards of job performance and to behave sensibly and safely at work. Discipline is essential to all organized group action.

Discipline is employee learning that promotes self-control, dedication, and orderly conduct. In relation to employees in the U.S., discipline is generally used in a restricted sense to mean punishment. Consequently, the written procedures used to punish employees for job deficiencies are called disciplinary procedures.

Punishment is the process of either administering an unpleasant stimulus, such as a warning letter or a suspension, or withholding a reward, such as not granting a scheduled pay increase because of an employee's job deficiencies. Punishment is only one form of discipline; other forms are positive reinforcement, including commendations and praise, and human resources development.

The first step is to establish and maintain a reasonable, but firm discipline line.

TOO HIGH - People are insulted. Productivity drops.

TOO LOW - People take liberties. Productivity drops.

Definition of Discipline

Discipline is a procedure that corrects or punishes a subordinate because a rule of procedure has been violated. · —Dessler,2001

Discipline should be viewed as a condition within an organisation whereby Employees know what is expected of them in terms of the organisation's rules, Standards and policies and what the consequences are of infractions. · —Rue & Byars, 1996.

According to Richard D. Calhoon, "*Discipline is the force that prompts individuals or groups to observe rules, regulations, standards and procedures deemed necessary for an organization.*"

Therefore discipline means securing consistent behaviour in accordance with the accepted norms of behaviour. I am sure you will agree that discipline is essential in every aspect of life. It is equally essential in industrial undertakings.

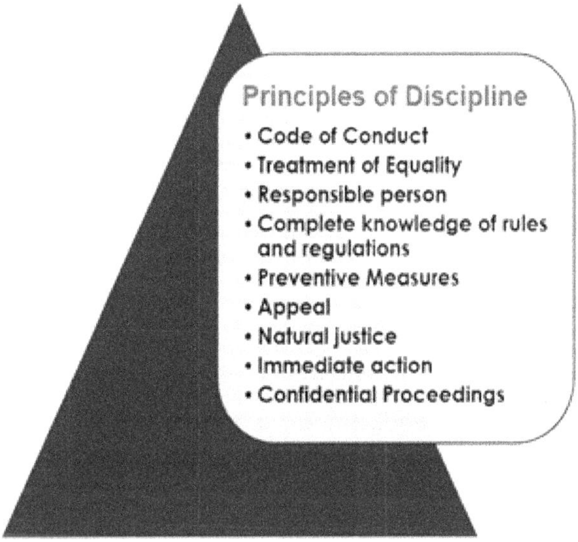

Features of Discipline

Discipline implies obedience, orderliness and maintenance of proper subordination among employees. Work recognition, fair and equitable treatment of employees, appropriate salary structure, effective grievance handling and job-security all contribute to organizational discipline.

Features of Discipline

3. Discipline is a negative approach in the sense that it encourages individual to undertake some actions that restrain them from undertaking others.
4. Discipline is a positive in the sense that it imposes a penalty if the values and norms that have been laid down by the organization are violated.

Significance of Discipline

Discipline is an approach used by management to modify undesirable performance and behavior through the use of a corrective action process. At the onset of any employee performance or conduct issues, supervisors are strongly encouraged to contact Employee Relations staff for assistance.

Types of Employee Discipline: Positive and Negative Discipline

The need for disciplinary action felt everywhere-be it at home, in the school, university or an organisation whenever one breaks the rules. Remember, either your own or some other children's behaviour in the shopping centre. You would have observed the various ways the parents use to discipline their rambunctious children in the shopping centers.

The three prominent ways are discussed below:

1. Some children well understand the proper behaviour expected of them in the shopping center and behave accordingly. They remain all the time stick to their parents. They neither touch, pull, push any item nor demand instantly for ice-cream, toy etc. Obviously, such children do not need to be disciplined. They gracefully accept no for an answer. Perhaps you were one of them.
2. You might have seen other children also treating the supermarket a place for fun and play, screaming and hollering, running up and down, here and there, and, thus, creating trouble for everyone concerned. Faced and annoyed with such behaviour, some parents react angrily, subjecting the child publicly to verbal and physical abuse.

These parents by shaking their fingers and fits try to sternly warn the sobbing child that repeated rowdiness will result in further stem punishments. The child has, thus, been struck with the fear of punishment, at least for the time being till in the shopping center.

3. Like your parents, other parents apply a different approach to discipline their children showing such inappropriate behaviour. They take calmly their child aside and clearly explain what type of behaviour is expected of them and how their misconduct creates problems and inconvenience to, other customers and shopkeepers.

Types of Discipline:

Action applied by managers.

1. Positive Discipline
2. Negative Discipline:

These are discussed one by one:

1. Positive Discipline:

This is also called 'self-imposed discipline'. It involves creation of an atmosphere in the organisation through rewards, appreciation, incentive payment, promotion, constructive support etc. to motivate employees to work willingly to accomplish the set goals.

In essence, positive discipline emphasises the concept of self-discipline or self-control. Thus, it reduces the need for personal supervision to make employees conform to organisational rules, regulations, procedures and standards.

According to William R. Spriegel, "Positive discipline does not replace reason but applies reason to the achievement of a common objective. Positive discipline does not restrict the individual but enables him to have a greater freedom in that he enjoys a greater degree of self-expression in striving to achieve the group objective, which he identifies as his own'"

Evidences suggest that self-disciplined person tends to be a better worker than one who is not. Self- discipline, when developed from within, leads to building up morale and esprit de corps that is the desideratum of the time to run organisations successfully.

2. Negative Discipline:

It is also called 'enforced discipline'. In case of negative discipline, employees are forced to obey orders and abide by rules and regulations that have been laid down, failing which penalties and punishment would be imposed on them. Thus, the objective of using punitive or coercive discipline is to ensure that employees do not violate rules and regulations formed by the organisation.

In other words, the purpose of negative discipline is to scare other employees and to ensure that they do not indulge in undesirable behaviour. It is worth mentioning here that negative discipline cannot eliminate the undesirable behaviour of the employees, but can merely suppress it.

Punishment is not pleasant. It causes resentment and hostility on the part of employees. That is why this kind of discipline results in only the minimum standards of performance on the part of employees. This is precisely the reason why it is rarely used in the organisations.

Because punitive discipline leads to resentment, it needs to be exercised in a progressive, sequential and chronological manner. A progressive system of discipline generally contains five steps, viz., an oral reprimand, a written reprimand, a second written warning, temporary suspension and dismissal or

Grievance

Employee Grievance is a formal complaint raised by an employee against a fellow employee or manager, or even against the employer. Employees usually file grievances for workplace harassment, discrimination, nepotism, concerns regarding team management or regarding terms of the employment.

Objectives and Benefits of Grievance Handling Procedure

The grievance procedure is the method by which a grievance is filed and carried through different steps to an ultimate decision.

Objectives of Grievance Handling Procedure:

1. To enable the employee to air their grievance
2. To clarify the nature of the grievance
3. To investigate the reasons for dissatisfaction
4. To obtain, where possible, a speedy resolution to the problem
5. To take appropriate actions and ensure that promises are kept:
6. To inform the employee of their right to take the grievance to the next stage of the procedure, in the event of an unsuccessful resolution

Grievance Handling Procedure:

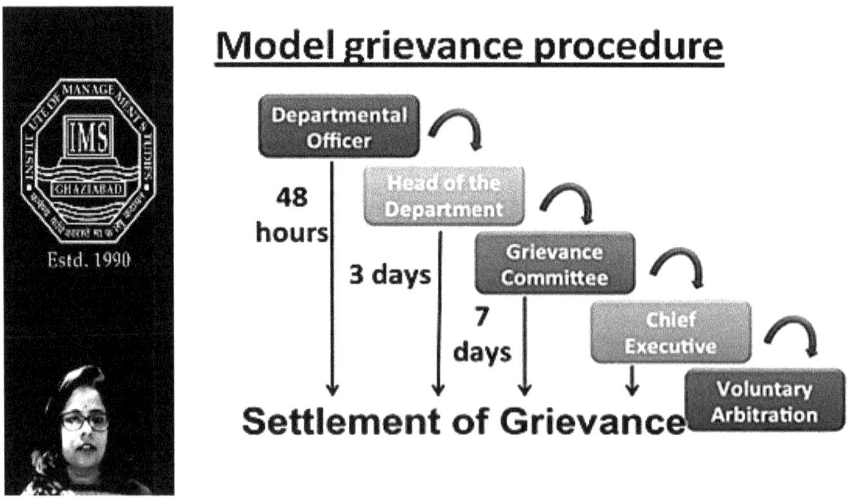

Benefits that accrue to both the employer and employees are as follows:

1. It encourages employees to raise concerns without fear of reprisal.
2. It provides a fair and speedy means of dealing with complaints.
3. It prevents minor disagreements developing into more serious disputes.
4. It serves as an outlet for employee frustrations and discontents.
5. It saves employer's time and money as solutions are found for workplace problems. It helps to build an organizational climate based on openness and trust.

Details of a grievance procedure/machinery may vary from organization to organization.

The four stages of the machinery are briefly discussed here:

1. Initial level at which grievance occurs:

The greatest opportunity to redress a grievance is to resolve it at the initial level at which it occurs. A worker's grievance should be resolved by their immediate boss, the first-line supervisor. The first stage of the procedure usually involves three persons—the aggrieved employee, his immediate boss and the union representative.

It is pos¬sible to involve the union in laying down the framework of the grievance procedure and thereaf¬ter restrain union involvement in the actual process, at least in the first two stages. Supervisory role needs to be strengthened, with appropriate training in problem-solving skills, grievance handling, and counselling.

2. Intermediate stage:

If the dispute is not redressed at the initial state at supervisor's level, it is usually referred to the head of the concerned department. It is important that the management assumes prime responsibility for the settlement of a grievance. At the intermediate level, griev¬ance can be settled with or without union involvement.

3. Organization level:

If a grievance is not settled at the intermediate level also, it can be referred to the top management. Usually, a person of a level not less than the general manager designated for the purpose directly handles the issue. At this level, it is very difficult to reconcile the con¬flicting interests.

4. Third-party mediation:

If the grievance has not been settled bilaterally within the organiza¬tion, it goes to a third party for mediation. Arbitration or adjudication or the matter may even be referred to a labour court. At this stage, the parties concerned lose control over the way the griev¬ance is settled.

In case of mediation (conciliation or arbitration), the mediator has no authority to decide, but in case of the labour court or an adjudicator, the decision will be binding on the parties, subject to statutory provisions for appeal to higher courts.

At any stage of the grievance machinery, the dispute must be handled by some members of the man¬agement. In grievance redressal, responsibility lies largely with the management. And, as already dis¬cussed, grievances should be settled promptly at the first stage itself.

Advertisements:

The following steps provide a measure of guidance to the manager dealing with grievances:

1. **Acknowledge dissatisfaction:**

   Managerial/supervisory attitude to grievances is important. They should focus attention on grievances, and not turn away from them. Ignorance is not bliss; it is the bane of industrial conflict. Arrogant attitude on the part of supervisors and managers aggravates the problem.

2. **Define the problem:**

   Instead of trying to deal with a vague feeling of discontent, the problem should be defined properly. Sometime the wrong complaint is given. By effective listening, one can make sure that a true complaint is voiced.

3. **Get the facts:**

   Facts should be separated from fiction. Although grievances result in hurt feelings, the effort should be to get the facts behind the feelings. There is need for a proper record of each grievance.

4. **Analyse and decide:**

   Decisions on each grievance will have a precedent effect. While no time should be lost in dealing with them, it is no excuse to be slipshod about it. Grievance settlements provide opportunities for managements to correct themselves, and thereby come closer to the employees. Horse-trading in grievance redressal due to union pressures may temporarily bring union leadership closer to the management, but it will surely alienate the workforce away from the management.

5. **Follow up:**

Decisions taken must be followed up earnestly. They should be promptly commu¬nicated to the concerned employee. If a decision is favourable to the employee, their immediate boss should have the privilege of communicating the same.

Trade Unions Act, 1926,

as amended

An Act to provide for the registration of Trade Unions and in certain respects to define the law relating to registered Trade Unions

Whereas it is expedient to provide for the registration of Trade Unions and in certain respects to define the law relating to registered Trade Unions;

It is hereby enacted as follows:

CHAPTER I - PRELIMINARY

1. Short title, extent and commencement.-

(1) This Act may be called the Trade Unions Act, 1926.

(2) It extends to the whole of India.

(3) It shall come into force on such date as the Central Government may, by notification in the Official Gazette, appoint.

2. Definitions.- In this Act 'the appropriate Government' means, in relation to Trade Unions whose objects are not confined to one State, the Central Government, and in relation to other Trade Unions, the State Government, and, unless there is anything repugnant in the subject or context, -

(a) "executive" means the body, by whatever name called, to which the management of the affairs of a Trade Union is entrusted;

(b) "office-bearer", in the case of a Trade Union, includes any member of the executive thereof, but does not include an auditor;

(c) "prescribed" means prescribed by regulations made under this Act;

(d) "registered office" means that office of a Trade Union which is registered under this Act as the head office thereof;

(e) "registered Trade Union" means a Trade Union registered under this Act;

(f) "Registrar" means -

(i) a Registrar of Trade Unions appointed by the appropriate Government under section 3, and includes any Additional or Deputy Registrar of Trade Unions; and

(ii) in relation to any Trade Union, the Registrar appointed for the State in which the head or registered office, as the case may be, of the Trade Union is situated ;

(g) "trade dispute" means any dispute between employers and workmen or between workmen and workmen, or between employers and employers which is connected with the employment or non-employment, or the terms of employment or the conditions of labour, of any person, and "workmen" means all persons employed in trade or industry whether or not in the employment of the employer with whom the trade dispute arises; and

(h) "Trade Union" means any combination, whether temporary or permanent, formed primarily for the purpose of regulating the relations between workmen and employers or between workmen and workmen, or between employers and employers, or for imposing restrictive conditions on the conduct of any trade or business, and includes any federation of two or more Trade Unions:

Provided that this Act shall not affect -

(i) any agreement between partners as to their own business;

(ii) any agreement between an employer and those employed by him as to such employment; or

(iii) any agreement in consideration of the sale of the good-will of a business or of instruction in any profession, trade or handicraft.

CHAPTER II - REGISTRATION OF TRADE UNIONS

3. Appointment of Registrars.-

(1) The appropriate Government shall appoint a person to be the Registrar of Trade Unions for each State.

(2) The appropriate Government may appoint as many Additional and Deputy Registrars of Trade Unions as it thinks fit for the purpose of exercising and discharging, under the superintendence and direction of the Registrar, such powers and functions of the Registrar under this Act as it may, by order, specify and define the local limits within which any such

Additional or Deputy Registrar shall exercise and discharge the powers and functions so specified.

(3) Subject to the provisions of any order under sub-section (2), where an Additional or Deputy Registrar exercises and discharges the powers and functions of a Registrar in an area within which the registered office of a Trade Union is situated, the Additional or Deputy Registrar shall be deemed to be the Registrar in relation to the Trade Union for the purposes of this Act.

4. Mode of registration.-

(1) Any seven or more members of a Trade Union may, by subscribing their names to the rules of the Trade Union and by otherwise complying with the provisions of this Act with respect to registration, apply for registration of the Trade Union under this Act.

(2) Where an application has been made under sub-section (1) for the registration of a Trade Union, such application shall not be deemed to have become invalid merely by reason of the fact that, at any time after the date of the application, but before the registration of the Trade Union, some of the applicants, but not exceeding half of the total number of persons who made the application, have ceased to be members of the Trade Union or have given notice in writing to the Registrar dissociating themselves from the application.

5. Application for registration.-

(1) Every application for registration of a Trade Union shall be made to the Registrar, and shall be accompanied by a copy of the rules of the Trade Union and a statement of the following particulars, namely: -

(a) the names, occupations and addresses of the members making the application;

(b) the name of the Trade Union and the address of its head office; and

(c) the titles, names, ages, addresses and occupations of the office-bearers of the Trade Union.

(2) Where a Trade Union has been in existence for more than one year before the making of an application for its registration, there shall be delivered to the Registrar, together with the application, a general statement of the assets and liabilities of the Trade Union prepared in such form and containing such particulars as may be prescribed.

6. Provisions to be contained in the rules of a Trade Union.- A Trade Union shall not be entitled to registration under this Act, unless the executive thereof is constituted in accordance with the provisions of this Act, and the rules thereof provide for the following matters, namely: -

(a) the name of the Trade Union;

(b) the whole of the objects for which the Trade Union has been established;

(c) the whole of the purposes for which the general funds of the Trade Union shall be applicable, all of which purposes shall be purposes to which such funds are lawfully applicable under this Act;

(d) the maintenance of a list of the members of the Trade Union and adequate facilities for the inspection thereof by the office-bearers and members of the Trade Union;

(e) the admission of ordinary members who shall be persons actually engaged or employed in an industry with which the Trade Union is connected, and also the admission of the number of honorary or temporary members as office-bearers required under section 22 to form the executive of the Trade Union;

(ee) the payment of a subscription by members of the Trade Union which shall be not less than twenty-five naye paise per month per member;

(f) the conditions under which any member shall be entitled to any benefit assured by the rules and under which any fine or forfeiture may be imposed on the members;

(g) the manner in which the rules shall be amended, varied or rescinded;

(h) the manner in which the members of the executive and the other office-bearers of the Trade Union shall be appointed and removed;

(i) the safe custody of the funds of the Trade Union, an annual audit, in such manner as may be prescribed, of the accounts thereof, and adequate facilities for the inspection of the account books by the office-bearers and members of the Trade Union; and

(j) the manner in which the Trade Union may be dissolved.

7. Power to call for further particulars and to require alteration of name.-

(1) The Registrar may call for further information for the purpose of satisfying himself that any application complies with the provisions of section 5, or that the Trade Union is entitled to registration under section 6, and may refuse to register the Trade Union until such information is supplied.

(2) If the name under which a Trade Union is proposed to be registered is identical with that by which any other existing Trade Union has been registered or, in the opinion of the Registrar, so nearly resembles such name as to be likely to deceive the public or the members of either Trade Union, the Registrar shall require the persons applying for registration to alter the name of the Trade Union stated in the application, and shall refuse to register the Union until such alteration has been made.

8. Registration.-The Registrar, on being satisfied that the Trade Union has complied with all the requirements of this Act in regard to registration, shall register the Trade Union by entering in a register, to be maintained in such form as may be prescribed, the particulars relating to the Trade Union contained in the statement accompanying the application for registration.

9. Certificate of registration.- The Registrar, on registering a Trade Union under section 8, shall issue a certificate of registration in the prescribed form which shall be conclusive evidence that the Trade Union has been duly registered under this Act.

10. Cancellation of registration.- A certificate of registration of a Trade Union may be withdrawn or cancelled by the Registrar -

(a) on the application of the Trade Union to be verified in such manner as may be prescribed, or

(b) if the Registrar is satisfied that the certificate has been obtained by fraud or mistake, or that the Trade Union has ceased to exist or has wilfully and after notice from the Registrar contravened any provision of this Act or allowed any rule to continue in force which is inconsistent with any such provision, or has rescinded any rule providing for any matter provision for which is required by section 6:

Provided that not less than two months' previous notice in writing specifying the ground on which it is proposed to withdraw or cancel the certificate shall be given by the Registrar to the Trade Union before the certificate is withdrawn or cancelled otherwise than on the application of the Trade Union.

11. Appeal.-

(1) Any person aggrieved by any refusal of the Registrar to register a Trade Union or by the withdrawal or cancellation of a certificate of registration may, within such period as may be prescribed, appeal,-

(a) where the head office of the Trade Union is situated within the limits of a Presidency-town, to the High Court, or

(b) where the head office is situated in any other area, to such Court, not inferior to the Court of an additional or assistant Judge of a principal Civil Court of original jurisdiction, as the appropriate Government may appoint in this behalf for that area.

(2) The appellate Court may dismiss the appeal, or pass an order directing the Registrar to register the Union and to issue a certificate of registration under the provisions of section 9 or setting aside the order for withdrawal or cancellation of the certificate, as the case may be, and the Registrar shall comply with such order.

(3) For the purpose of an appeal under sub-section (1) an appellate Court shall, so far as may be, follow the same procedure and have the same powers as it follows and has when trying a suit under the Code of Civil Procedure,

1908 (5 of 1908), and may direct by whom the whole or any part of the costs of the appeal shall be paid, and such costs shall be recovered as if they had been awarded in a suit under the said Code.

(4) In the event of the dismissal of an appeal by any Court appointed under clause (b) of sub-section (1), the person aggrieved shall have a right of appeal to the High Court, and the High Court shall, for the purpose of such appeal, have all the powers of an appellate Court under sub-sections (2) and (3), and the provisions of those sub-sections shall apply accordingly.

12. Registered office.- All communications and notices to a registered Trade Union may be addressed to its registered office. Notice of any change in the address of the head office shall be given within fourteen days of such change to the Registrar in writing, and the changed address shall be recorded in the register referred to in section 8.

13. Incorporation of registered Trade Unions.- Every registered Trade Union shall be a body corporate by the name under which it is registered, and shall have perpetual succession and a common seal with power to acquire and hold both movable and immovable property and to contract, and shall by the said name sue and be sued.

14. Certain Acts not to apply to registered Trade Unions.- The following Acts, namely: -

(a) The Societies Registration Act, 1860 (21 of 1860),

(b) The Co-operative Societies Act, 1912 (2 of 1912),

(c) The Companies Act, 1956 (1 of 1956);

shall not apply to any registered Trade Union, and the registration of any such Trade Union under any such Act shall be void.

CHAPTER III - RIGHTS AND LIABILITIES OF REGISTERED TRADE UNIONS

15. Objects on which general funds may be spent.- The general funds of a registered Trade Union shall not be spent on any other objects than the following, namely: -

(a) the payment of salaries, allowances and expenses to office-bearers of the Trade Union;

(b) the payment of expenses for the administration of the Trade Union, including audit of the accounts of the general funds of the Trade Union;

(c) the prosecution or defence of any legal proceeding to which the Trade Union or any member thereof is a party, when such prosecution or defence is undertaken for the purpose of securing or protecting any rights of the Trade Union as such or any rights arising out of the relations of any member with his employer or with a person whom the member employs;

(d) the conduct of trade disputes on behalf of the Trade Union or any member thereof;

(e) the compensation of members for loss arising out of trade disputes;

(f) allowances to members or their dependants on account of death, old age, sickness, accidents or unemployment of such members;

(g) the issue of, or the undertaking of liability under, policies of assurance on the lives of members, or under policies insuring members against sickness, accident or unemployment;

(h) the provision of educational, social or religious benefits for members (including the payment of the expenses of funeral or religious ceremonies for deceased members) or for the dependants of members;

(i) the upkeep of a periodical published mainly for the purpose of discussing questions affecting employers or workmen as such;

(j) the payment, in furtherance of any of the objects on which the general funds of the Trade Union may be spent, of contributions to any cause intended to benefit workmen in general, provided that the expenditure in respect of such contributions in any financial year shall not at any time during that year be in excess of one-fourth of the combined total of the gross income which has up to that time accrued to the general funds of the Trade Union during that year and of the balance at the credit of those funds at the commencement of that year; and

(k) subject to any conditions contained in the notification, any other object notified by the appropriate Government in the official Gazette.

16. Constitution of a separate fund for political purposes.-

(1) A registered Trade Union may constitute a separate fund, from contributions separately levied for or made to that fund, from which payments may be made, for the promotion of the civic and political interests of its members, in furtherance of any of the objects specified in sub-section (2).

(2) The objects referred to in sub-section (1) are: -

(a) the payment of any expenses incurred, either directly or indirectly, by a candidate or prospective candidate for election as a member of any legislative body constituted under the Constitution or of any local authority, before, during, or after the election in connection with his candidature or election; or

(b) the holding of any meeting or the distribution of any literature or documents in support of any such candidate or prospective candidate; or

(c) the maintenance of any person who is a member of any legislative body constituted under the Constitution or of any local authority; or

(d) the registration of electors or the election of a candidate for any legislative body constituted under the Constitution or for any local authority; or

(e) the holding of political meetings of any kind, or the distribution of political literature or political documents of any kind.

(2A) In its application to the State of Jammu and Kashmir, references in sub-section (2) to any legislative body constituted under the Constitution shall be construed as including references to the Legislature of that State.

(3) No member shall be compelled to contribute to the fund constituted under sub-section (1); and a member who does not contribute to the said fund shall not be excluded from any benefits of the Trade Union, or placed in any respect either directly or indirectly under any disability or at any disadvantage as compared with other members of the Trade Union (except in relation to the control or management of the said fund) by reason of his not contributing to the said fund; and contribution to the said fund shall not be made a condition for admission to the Trade Union.

17. Criminal conspiracy in trade disputes.- No office-bearer or member of a registered Trade Union shall be liable to punishment under sub-section (2) of section 120B Indian Penal Code (45 of 1860), in respect of any agreement made between the members for the purpose of furthering any such object of the Trade Union as is specified in section 15, unless the agreement is an agreement to commit an offence.

18. Immunity from civil suit in certain cases.-

(1) No suit or other legal proceeding shall be maintainable in any Civil Court against any registered Trade Union or any office-bearer; or member thereof in respect of any act done in contemplation or furtherance of a trade dispute to which a member of the Trade Union is a party on the ground only that such act induces some other person to break a contract of employment, or that it is in interference with the trade, business or employment of some other person or with the right of some other person to dispose of his capital or of his labour as he wills.

(2) A registered Trade Union shall not be liable in any suit or other legal proceeding in any Civil Court in respect of any tortious act done in contemplation or furtherance of a trade dispute by an agent of the Trade Union if it is proved that such person acted without the knowledge of, or contrary to express instructions given by, the executive of the Trade Union.

19. Enforceability of agreements.- Notwithstanding anything contained in any other law for the time being in force, an agreement between the members

of a registered Trade Union shall not be void or voidable merely by reason of the fact that any of the objects of the agreement are in restraint of trade:

Provided that nothing in this section shall enable any Civil Court to entertain any legal proceeding instituted for the express purpose of enforcing or recovering damages for the breach of any agreement concerning the conditions on which any members of a Trade Union shall or shall not sell their goods, transact business, work, employ or be employed.

20. Right to inspect books of Trade Union.- The account books of a registered Trade Union and the list of members thereof shall be open to inspection by an office-bearer or member of the Trade Union at such times as may be provided for in the rules of the Trade Union.

21. Rights of minors to membership of Trade Unions.- Any person who has attained the age of fifteen years may be a member of a registered Trade Union subject to any rules of the Trade Union to the contrary, and may, subject as aforesaid, enjoy all the rights of a member and execute all instruments and give all acquittances necessary to be executed or given under the rules.

21A. Disqualifications of office-bearers of Trade Unions.-

(1) A person shall be disqualified for being chosen as, and for being, a member of the executive or any other office-bearer of a registered Trade Union if -

    (i) he has not attained the age of eighteen years,

    (ii) he has been convicted by a Court in India of any offence involving moral turpitude and sentenced to imprisonment, unless a period of five years has elapsed since his release.

(2) Any member of the executive or other office-bearer of a registered Trade Union who, before the commencement of the Indian Trade Unions (Amendment) Act, 1964 (38 of 1964), has been convicted of any offence involving moral turpitude and sentenced to imprisonment, shall on the date of such commencement cease to be such member or office-bearer unless a period of five years has elapsed since his release before that date.

(3) In its application to the State of Jammu and Kashmir, reference in sub-section (2) to the commencement of the Indian Trade Unions (Amendment) Act, 1964 (38 of 1964), shall be construed as reference to the commencement of this Act in the said State.

22. Proportion of office-bearers to be connected with the industry.- Not less than one-half of the total number of the office-bearers of every registered Trade Union shall be persons actually engaged or employed in an industry with which the Trade Union is connected:

Provided that the appropriate Government may, by special or general order, declare that the provisions of this section shall not apply to any Trade Union or class of Trade Unions specified in the order.

23. Change of name.- Any registered Trade Union may, with the consent of not less than two-thirds of the total number of its members and subject to the provisions of section 25, change its name.

24. Amalgamation of Trade Unions.- Any two or more registered Trade Unions may become amalgamated together as one Trade Union with or without dissolution or division of the funds of such Trade Unions or either or any of them, provided that the votes of at least one-half of the members of each or every such trade Union entitled to vote are recorded, and that at least sixty per cent of the votes recorded are in favour of the proposal.

25. Notice of change of name or amalgamation.-

(1) Notice in writing of every change of name of every amalgamation, signed, in the case of a change of name, by the Secretary and by seven members of the Trade Union changing its name, and, in the case of an amalgamation, by the Secretary and by seven members of each and every Trade Union which is a party thereto, shall be sent to the Registrar, and where the head office of the amalgamated Trade Union is situated in a different State, to the Registrar of such State.

(2) If the proposed name is identical with that by which any other existing Trade Union has been registered or, in the opinion of the Registrar, so nearly resembles such name as to be likely to deceive the public or the members of either Trade Union, the Registrar shall refuse to register the change of name.

(3) Save as provided in sub-section (2), the Registrar shall, if he is satisfied that the provisions of this Act in respect of change of name have been complied with, register the change of name in the register referred to in section 8, and the change of name shall have effect from the date of such registration.

(4) The Registrar of the State in which the head office of the amalgamated Trade Union is situated shall, if he is satisfied that the provisions of this Act in respect of amalgamation have been complied with and that the Trade Union formed thereby is entitled to registration under section 6, register the Trade Union in the manner provided in section 8, and the amalgamation shall have effect from the date of such registration.

26. Effects of change of name and of amalgamation.-

(1) The change in the name of a registered Trade Union shall not a affect any rights or obligations of the Trade Union or render defective any legal proceeding by or against the Trade Union, and any legal proceeding which might have been continued or commenced by or against it by its former name may be continued or commenced by or against it by its new name.

(2) An amalgamation of two or more registered Trade Unions shall not prejudice any right of any of such Trade Unions or any right of a creditor of any of them.

27. Dissolution.-

(1) When a registered Trade Union is dissolved, notice of the dissolution signed by seven members and by the Secretary of the Trade Union shall, within fourteen days of the dissolution, be sent to the Registrar, and shall be registered by him if he is satisfied that the dissolution has been effected in accordance with the rules of the Trade Union, and the dissolution shall have effect from the date of such registration.

(2) Where the dissolution of a registered Trade Union has been registered and the rules of the Trade Union do not provide for the distribution of funds of the Trade Union on dissolution, the Registrar shall divide the funds amongst the members in such manner as may be prescribed.

28. Returns.-

(1) There shall be sent annually to the Registrar, on or before such date as may be prescribed, a general statement, audited in the prescribed manner, of all receipts and expenditure of every registered Trade Union during the year ending on the 31st day of December next preceding such prescribed date, and of the assets and liabilities of the Trade Union existing on such 31st day of December. The statement shall be prepared in such form and shall comprise such particulars as may be prescribed.

(2) Together with the general statement there shall be sent to the Registrar a statement showing all changes of office-bearers made by the Trade Union during the year to which the general statement refers, together also with a copy of the rules of the Trade Union corrected up to the date of the despatch thereof to the Registrar.

(3) A copy of every alteration made in the rules of a registered Trade Union shall be sent to the Registrar within fifteen days of the making of the alteration.

(4) For the purpose of examining the documents referred to in sub-sections (1), (2) and (3), the Registrar, or any officer authorised by him, by general or special order, may at all reasonable times inspect the certificate of registration, account books, registers, and other documents, relating to a Trade Union, at its registered office or may require their production at such place as he may specify in this behalf, but no such place shall be at a distance of more than ten miles from the registered office of a Trade Union.

CHAPTER IV - REGULATIONS

29. Power to make regulations.-

(1) The appropriate Government may make regulations for the purpose of carrying into effect the provisions of this Act.

(2) In particular and without prejudice to the generality of the foregoing power, such regulations may provide for all or any of the following matters, namely: -

  (a) the manner in which Trade Unions and the rules of Trade Unions shall be registered and the fees payable on registration;

  (b) the transfer of registration in the case of any registered Trade Union which has changed its head office from one State to another;

  (c) the manner in which, and the qualifications of persons by whom, the accounts of registered Trade Unions or of any class of such Unions shall be audited;

  (d) the conditions subject to which inspection of documents kept by Registrars shall be allowed and the fees which shall be chargeable in respect of such inspections; and

  (e) any matter which is to be or may be prescribed.

30. Publication of regulations.-

(1) The power to make regulations conferred by section 29 is subject to the condition of the regulations being made after previous publication.

(2) The date to be specified in accordance with clause (3) of section 23 of the General Clauses Act, 1897 (10 of 1897), as that after which a draft of regulations proposed to be made will be taken into consideration shall not be less than three months from the date on which the draft of the proposed regulations was published for general information.

(3) Regulations so made shall be published in the Official Gazette, and on such publication shall have effect as if enacted in this Act.

CHAPTER V - PENALTIES AND PROCEDURE

32. Supplying false information regarding Trade Unions.- Any person who, with intent to deceive, gives to any member of a registered Trade Union or to any person intending or applying to become a member of such Trade Union any document purporting to be a copy of the rules of the Trade Union or of any alterations to the same which he knows, or has reason to believe, is not a correct copy of such rules or alterations as are for the time being in force, or any person who, with the like intent, gives a copy of any rules of an unregistered Trade Union to any person on the pretence that

such rules are the rules of a registered Trade Union, shall be punishable with fine which may extend to two hundred rupees.

31. Failure to submit returns.-

(1) If default is made on the part of any registered Trade Union in giving any notice or sending any statement or other document as required by or under any provision of this Act, every office-bearer or other person bound by the rules of the Trade Union to give or send the same, or, if there is no such office-bearer or person every member of the executive of the Trade Union, shall be punishable, with fine which may extend to five rupees and, in the case of a continuing default, with an additional fine which may extend to five rupees for each week after the first during which the default continues:

Provided that the aggregate fine shall not exceed fifty rupees.

(2) Any person who wilfully makes, or causes to be made, any false entry in, or any omission from, the general statement required by section 28, or in or from any copy of rules or of alterations of rules sent to the Registrar under that section, shall be punishable with fine which may extend to five hundred rupees.

32. Supplying false information regarding Trade Unions.- Any person who, with intent to deceive, gives to any member of a registered Trade Union or to any person intending or applying to become a member of such Trade Union any document purporting to be a copy of the rules of the Trade Union or of any alterations to the same which he knows, or has reason to believe, is not a correct copy of such rules or alterations as are for the time being in force, or any person who, with the like intent, gives a copy of any rules of an unregistered Trade Union to any person on the pretence that such rules are the rules of a registered Trade Union, shall be punishable with fine which may extend to two hundred rupees.

33. Cognizance of offences.-

(1) No Court inferior to that of a Presidency Magistrate or a Magistrate of the first class shall try any offence under this Act.

(2) No Court shall take cognizance of any offence under this Act, unless complaint thereof has been made by, or with the previous sanction of, the Registrar or, in the case of an offence under section 32, by the person to whom the copy was given, within six months of the date on which the offence is alleged to have been committed.

Trade Union-

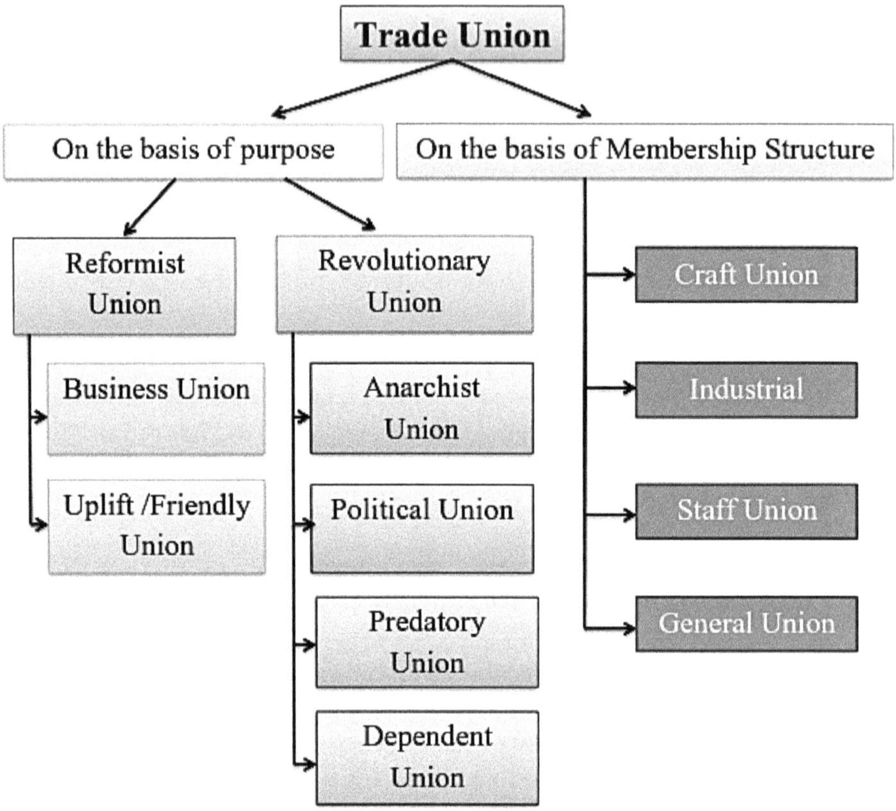

A trade union is an organisation made up of members (a membership-based organisation) and its membership must be made up mainly of workers. One of a trade union's main aims is to protect and advance the interests of its members in the workplace. Most trade unions are independent of any employer.

Type Of Trade Union-

Problems of Trade Unions

- Uneven Growth. Trade unions are concentrated in large scale industry sector and in big industrial centers. ...
- Small Size. ...
- Weak Financial Position. ...
- Political Leadership. ..
- Multiplicity of Unions.

www.ingramcontent.com/pod-product-compliance
Ingram Content Group UK Ltd.
Pitfield, Milton Keynes, MK11 3LW, UK
UKHW021406190726
13845UKWH00028B/914

9 789358 988932